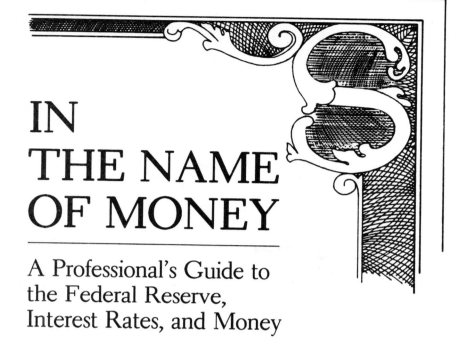

IN
THE NAME
OF MONEY

A Professional's Guide to the Federal Reserve, Interest Rates, and Money

PAUL DeROSA
Vice President
Citibank, N. A.

GARY H. STERN
Senior Economist
A. Gary Shilling & Co., Inc.

McGraw-Hill Book Company

New York   St. Louis   San Francisco   Auckland
Bogotá   Hamburg   Johannesburg   London   Madrid
Montreal   New Delhi   Panama   Paris   São Paulo
Singapore   Sydney   Tokyo   Toronto   Mexico

Library of Congress Cataloging in Publication Data

DeRosa, Paul.
  In the name of money.

  1. United States. Board of Governors of the
Federal Reserve System. 2. Monetary policy—United
States. 3. Interest and usury—United States.
I. Stern, Gary H., joint author. II. Title.
HG2563.D43   332.4'973   80-18534
ISBN 0-07-016521-1

1234567890   DODO   8987654321

The editors for this book were Kiril Sokoloff and
Virginia Fechtmann Blair, the designer was Mark E. Safran, and
the production supervisor was Thomas G. Kowalczyk. It was set
in Electra by University Graphics, Incorporated.

Printed and bound by R. R. Donnelly & Sons Company.

To, for, and in spite of Charles, Matthew,
Merideth, and Stephen

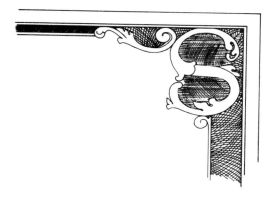

Contents

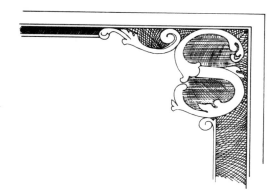

Introduction

To the investor in the United States, the Federal Reserve is a constant fascination. It is a large, powerful, active organization, whose policies direct the course of finance and determine the fates of numerous undertakings. Yet, to study the Federal Reserve is also to learn frustration. Like the CIA, it keeps secrets. Its operation is complex, its intentions are difficult to read, and its language is foreign to the ear. As one might expect, this combination has made the central bank the subject of an enormous literature that ranges in content from pure theory to near fiction.

The interested reader has little trouble staying informed on the large issues of monetary policy. The financial press contains a running commentary on the Federal Reserve's ties to the White House, its role in recycling oil payments, or the latest moves in the fight against inflation. People are justifiably concerned over the strategy of monetary policy and feel they have a right, even a duty, to offer free advice. Investors also have a stake in these matters because the values of equities and bonds obviously depend upon inflation, employment, and exchange rates. Yet, a general knowledge of monetary policy will not alone sustain the professional investor.

During nearly every week, the Federal Reserve does something that affects short-term interest rates and alters the basis for financial decisions. Few of these actions are motivated by concern for inflation, unemployment, or any other cosmic objective. Most of them seek a relatively immediate goal, like the adjustment of member bank reserves or the provision of currency during the month of December. The Federal Reserve assumes that market professionals know what the Fed is doing and accepts no responsibility to explain its intention. To the person who knows only that policy is somehow tight or easy, these open-market operations are disquieting. They appear arbitrary and unrelated to the central bank's ultimate purpose. Or what is worse, they suggest a change in policy or the arrival into the market of new information of which the person is unaware.

There is much more than temporary peace of mind to be gained from close study of the Federal Reserve, however. Over the years, the central bank has become notorious for a lack of candor about its own intentions, and fortunes have been won or lost on the ability to assess the consequences of monetary policy.

Officially the Federal Reserve has been fighting inflation for 15 years, but inflation has become only worse. In 1976, an important Wall Street economist predicted a 20-year bull market in bonds largely because Arthur Burns had sworn to hold down the money supply. The same man later became one of the most outspoken bears in American finance as he perceived a growing inconsistency between the Federal Reserve's word and its actions. As a result of this switch, he probably saved both his firm and its clients millions of dollars, and this was achieved not through any deep research but from an ability to measure the strengths and shortcomings of the central bank.

The reader of this book is unlikely to join the ranks of Fed-watchers and financial gurus, but he or she could become less dependent upon them. The reader will find in it a large amount of plain factual information on how the Federal Reserve carries out its policies and about the immediate effects of Federal Reserve operations upon the financial markets. Wherever possible, the book shuns the theoretical and concentrates on the factual, but some theory is unavoidable. The Federal Reserve does not act arbitrarily. It has in mind a conceptual framework that relates the things it does to the world it seeks to affect. The Federal Reserve uses theory at essentially two levels—first, as a bridge between control of the money supply and its objectives for price inflation and economic growth and, second, to forecast the influence of its open market operations upon the money supply. Anyone seeking to understand the Federal Reserve cannot escape some study of these matters.

Most of the theoretical material is confined to Chapter 1, where we discuss the strategic considerations of monetary policy. The Federal Reserve's ultimate purpose is to promote smooth noninflationary economic growth. It attempts to do this by controlling the rate at which the money supply is allowed to grow. Chapter 1 outlines the principal arguments for basing a stabilization policy upon the money supply and for preferring it to alternative instruments that could be employed.

The Federal Reserve is necessarily more preoccupied with the implementation of monetary policy than with its design. Having decided upon a desirable rate of monetary growth, it must somehow bring that growth about. The Federal Reserve does not itself issue money. It has direct control only over its portfolio of U.S. government and agency securities, which it manipulates in the hope of influencing the money supply. These efforts and their effects upon short-term interest rates are the subjects of Chapters 2 and 3. The market that feels the impact of central bank operations first is the Federal funds market, which is the place large financial institutions exchange very short term loans. Chapter 2 describes the structure of the Federal funds market, the forces that determine the interest rate on Federal funds loans, and the effects of Federal Reserve operations upon the market's equilibrium. Chapter 3 builds on this information and integrates it with the strategy for regulating money.

Chapter 4 generalizes the discussion of Federal funds and introduces the markets for other short-term financial instruments. This material elucidates the role of money market instruments in the fund-raising efforts of commercial banks and other financial intermediaries and in the cash management problems of corporations. Chapter 5 delves into the relationship between the Federal funds rate and other money market yields. This discussion is necessarily speculative, for interest rates, even short-term ones, are strongly influenced by the public's expectations of future events, which are themselves not susceptible to discrete analysis. Nevertheless, the chapter draws upon recent economic research as well as the authors' own experience in the financial markets to outline several considerations that have provided insights into the movements of interest rates.

Chapter 6 deals with the issues of how monetary policy affects jobs and spending. It closes the circle by elaborating on the questions of strategy that are introduced in Chapter 1. The literature on the relationship between monetary policy and the pace of business is enormous, and we can do little more than summarize a few of the important points. Every public policy that is honestly made rests upon some theory that relates the action taken to the goal that is sought. Our aim is to convey some sense of what might be expected from monetary policy. Chapter 7 discusses the international aspects of Federal Reserve operations and the constraints that are imposed upon domestic policy by concern for the exchange rate. Ten years ago this book would not have needed a Chapter 7; now one could argue it should comprise nearly half. Our aim here is twofold—to describe what the Federal Reserve does in the international markets and to weigh the importance of international issues for monetary policy.

Chapter 8 summarizes the first seven chapters. We expect that readers may want to return to the book after an initial review, using it as a handbook when they need information about the Federal Reserve. Chapter 8 provides a refresher course on the book's principal themes. The text is written throughout with a professional reader in mind, so many technical terms are used in the text without definition. However, the reader who does know what a bankers' acceptance is or has never heard the term "overnight repo" need not be dismayed. There is a glossary at the end of the last chapter.

Books like this one usually have no need of footnotes or references because they are obviously derivative and lay no claim to intellectual novelty. However, we would like to acknowledge at least a few of our debts. Much of the material in Chapter 1, on the historical and cyclical relationships between money and national income, comes from *The Monetary History of the United States*, by Milton Friedman and Anna J. Schwartz. Readers interested in these matters could do no better than to pursue them in the Friedman and Schwartz volume. Also, in Chapter 4, a large part of the analysis of financial intermediaries is based on work by Stanley Diller, in his essay "Credit Allocation and Housing" that was published in a volume entitled *Issues in Financial Regulation*. On more mundane matters, we would like to thank our former colleague at the Federal Reserve Bank of New York, Frederick J. Levin, for his thoughtful comments on an early draft of the book; C. J. DeRosa, who served ably as an unpaid research assistant to his dad; and colleagues at A. Gary Shilling and Company for several stimulating suggestions.

The Aims and Methods of Monetary Policy

Introduction

Imagine trying to explain the Federal Reserve System to a Martian, who had not read Professor Samuelson's textbook while at college. Consider the grandeur of the system's aspirations: attempting to smooth the fluctuations in a $2½ trillion economy, assure the jobs of 100 million people, combat price inflation, regulate 5000 commercial banks, and manage the rates of exchange between the dollar and about a dozen other currencies. Contrast this with the parsimony of its means. For all the powers that nominally reside in the central bank, the one identifiable act in which it regularly engages is the purchase and sale of government securities. A polite Martian would suppress a smile, but only by an act of faith could it accept a system that promises so much from doing so little. Nor would the Martian's doubts be assuaged by an appeal to the Federal Reserve's record of performance over the past two decades, which shows four recessions, a fivefold increase in the rate of inflation, and a 20 percent decline in the value of the dollar against most foreign currencies.

The Federal Reserve Act of 1914 and the Banking Act of 1933 endow the central bank with several market and regulatory powers, besides the ability to conduct open market operations, but many of them are of little consequence or are rarely employed. For example, there was once a time, some years ago, when banks relied heavily

1

upon funds borrowed from the Federal Reserve, and the discount rate was an essential component of monetary policy. More recently, banks obtain only a minuscule fraction of their funds at the discount window, and the rate has no influence upon their loan pricing. Discounting has fallen into such insignificance that many economists suggest the Federal Reserve discontinue the practice.

The Federal Reserve also can establish the reserves that 5000 of the nation's 14,000 banks must hold against deposits. An increase in reserve ratios reduces the portion of each deposit dollar that banks can relend and raises the cost of bank credit relative to loans from other sources. When most borrowers got their loans from banks, reserve ratios were important, but they have become much less so with the development of thrift institutions, finance companies, the commercial paper market, and other forms of nonbank credit. Member banks have become increasingly resentful of higher reserve ratios because they realize that their main effect is to rechannel credit flows around the banking system, with little change in the total. This has led to a membership problem and has made the Federal Reserve reluctant to alter reserve requirements in any circumstances short of crisis.

The central bank also can apply something called moral suasion. One never knows if moral suasion ever was an effective policy tool, or if it is one of those things that always worked better in days gone by. Whichever it is, from time to time, the chairman of the Federal Reserve gathers together the leaders of the major banks, lectures them on social responsibility, and exacts certain concessions under the implied threat of more regulation. These requests for good behavior are temporary and, in the past, have had negligible effects upon economic events.

For its international operations, the Federal Reserve controls large amounts of foreign currencies and can obtain additional amounts by exercising its swap lines with central banks in other countries. In a swap, the other bank gets a dollar deposit at the Federal Reserve, and the Federal Reserve receives an equivalent amount in foreign currency. The combination of swaps and other facilities gives the Federal Reserve $30 billion worth of funds, which it can use to support the dollar's exchange rate in international markets. Such salvage operations can raise the dollar's value for short periods of time, but experience has shown that, at most, these efforts are ancillary to broader policies against inflation, upon which the value of the dollar ultimately depends.

Officials of the Federal Reserve would not deny that open market operations in Treasury securities are, day in and day out, the substance of monetary policy. Yet most of them prefer to look a step or two beyond these activities. For the Federal Reserve, the unit of design in monetary policy is the growth rate of the nation's money stock. Restrictive policy, which intends to reduce the rate of economic growth, is, by definition, slower-growing money. Stimulative policy is faster money growth. Open market operations are the means by which the money supply is regulated. In order to bridge the gap between its portfolio of securities, which is the one quantity over which it has complete control, and economic growth and inflation, which are the things it aspires to influence, the Federal Reserve has constructed a hierarchy of intermediate objectives. These include bank reserves, the interest rate on Federal funds, the money supply, and finally the gross national product. At least 90 percent of the central bank's daily activities consist of purchases and sales of Treasury securities. These operations are the immediate point of contact between monetary policy and the markets for financial assets. They alter the supply and demand for Treasury securities, and they affect member bank reserves and market interest rates. Yet the patterns of open market operations and of resultant changes in interest rates are unintelligible without reference to the Federal Reserve's plans for the money stock and to its objectives for the national income, employment, and the rate of price inflation.

The Importance of Money

Scholars of intellectual history have found that as a rule it takes some 20 years from the time an idea is accepted among specialists in any field until it becomes the basis for public policy. The example of industrial regulation supports this hypothesis. Economists generally agreed by the early 1960s that most industrial regulation was at best useless, but it was not until Congress restored price competition to the airline industry in 1978 that the deregulation of the American economy was begun. In the case of economic stabilization policy, the process worked much faster. The argument for basing a monetary policy on the money supply jelled sometime around 1965, and within six years the Federal Reserve began explicit efforts to track monetary growth. The speed with which "aggregates policy," as the Federal Reserve has named it, was adopted is more surprising considering the low esteem in which the money supply was so recently held. As late as 1940 the vast majority of economists and government officials agreed that monetary and financial factors could influence neither the pace of business nor the rate of price inflation. Statistics on the money supply were collected and published in the Federal Reserve's monthly *Bulletin*, but they were mostly ignored. The Federal Reserve itself was assigned no role in economic stabilization. Its job was to hold down interest rates to minimize the tax burden of financing the national debt.

From that point there began a reassessment of monetary policy and of the importance of the money supply. The process continued unevenly for nearly three decades, culminating around 1970, with the Federal Reserve in almost sole charge of countercyclical economic policy and using the money supply as its instrument of control. The changes of the intervening 30 years were motivated, first, by the world of practical experience. Countries that consciously held down interest rates found themselves disarmed before inflation and were forced to let rates rise. The United States, after two years of inflation, gave up the effort in 1951, when the Treasury released the Federal Reserve from its assignment of supporting the price of Government bonds. Germany went through a similar experience after the war and reformed its monetary system in 1949, and England followed a few years later. Among professional economists, men like Gottfried Haberler, Albert Pigou, and, later, Arthur Burns and Milton Friedman worked to overcome the super-Keynesian bias in American economic thought. Besides arguing on points of theory, these men attacked the American Keynesians on the grounds that Keynes himself favored an active central bank. Influenced by the Great Depression, the Americans had caricatured Keynes by concentrating on periods of economic collapse and treating them as the normal state of affairs, when Keynes clearly recognized they were rare events.

More than any other person, Milton Friedman has come to be identified with the present approach to monetary management in the United States, and in other countries as well. He undoubtedly would disavow responsibility for its specific application, but to the extent that any coherent model guides the central bank, it is the outcome of Friedman's research and teaching. His thought is reflected also in the government's attempts to aid the underprivileged, redesign the system of public education, and deregulate industry. Indeed, for a person who never has held an official position, Friedman is remarkable in American history for the breadth of his influence. But he is best known for having assembled, either personally or through followers, the body of evidence that led the Federal Reserve to found its policy on control of the money supply.

Money and Inflation

For the person without formal training in economics, the relationship between money and economic conditions is not obvious. It isn't completely obvious for many people with training in economics, and several of its aspects still are the subjects of a lively debate. However, most students of the field agree that over a period of several years there is a close association between the rate of growth in the money supply and the rate of price inflation. In most countries, throughout history, lasting increases in the growth rate of money have been accompanied by faster-rising prices, and shortages of money have coincided with falling prices. This has been true regardless of whether the medium of exchange was gold coins, paper currency, or pounds of salt. It also is independent of the form of economic organization. Too much money caused as much inflation in precapitalist Europe as it has in modern socialist and free-enterprise economies.

In the United States since 1867, there have been three sustained periods of inflation—1914 to 1920, 1939 to 1948, and 1967 through 1979. During each of these periods, the money supply grew faster than it did during any other interval of similar duration. In the seven years beginning with 1914, the sum of currency, demand deposits, and savings deposits at commercial banks expanded at a 12 percent annual rate. Between 1939 and 1948, it grew at a 13 percent rate, and in the 14 years after 1965, it increased at over a 10 percent rate. Each of these periods also included a major war, and some part of the price increases could reasonably be attributed to wartime conditions. Nevertheless, the money supply did grow rapidly during each of them, and the continuation of high inflation for at least 10 years beyond the end of the Vietnam conflict renders the explanation of war effects implausible in this instance.

Since 1863, there have been four periods of reasonably stable prices. These were 1882 to 1892, 1903 to 1913, 1923 to 1929, and 1948 to 1963. The last period was interrupted by a burst of inflation in 1950, but that was brief and obviously a result of the Korean war. The average rate of increase in the money supply during the stable price periods was a touch under 5 percent, and during the longest interval, from 1948 until 1963, money grew at barely more than a 3 percent rate.

The United States has experienced but one episode of falling prices of any consequence in the last 117 years, and that one lasted only from 1930 through 1933. This period also witnessed an enormous contraction in the money supply. From July 1929 to March 1933, the nation suffered its worst financial collapse since the panic of 1837, and the money supply declined by nearly 40 percent.

Money and Business Cycles

These few facts are a small sample of the evidence documenting the long-run relationship between money and prices. They strongly imply that the Federal Reserve can control the secular trend of prices by limiting growth in the stock of money. However, these data do not address the question of whether the central bank can do more than regulate the long-run inflation rate. The average rate of price increase can be very near to zero, but if that average consists of alternating periods of 10 percent inflation and 10 percent deflation, few people would be satisfied with the economy's performance. Over time increasing demands have been placed upon the Federal Reserve to stabilize the fluctuations in real income and prices over relatively brief business cycles. These demands generally have been encouraged by demonstrations of the close short-run relationship between money and economic conditions. For example, in columns (1) and (4) of Table 1-1 are listed the dates of the peaks and troughs of the business cycles in the United States between 1908 and 1960. In columns (2) and (5) are the dates of peaks and troughs of the growth rate of the money supply. Money is measured here as the total of demand deposits, time and savings accounts, and currency in the hands of the public—the old definition of M-2. Columns (3) and (6) list the number of months between the turning points of M-2 growth and corresponding turns in economic activity. Of the 12 business peaks, 10 either coincided with or were preceded by a sharp decline in the growth rate of M-2. Of the 13 troughs, 11 either coincided with or followed an acceleration in the growth of M-2. At the peaks, the average time between the drop of money growth and the economic slump was 8.1 months. At the troughs the corresponding lag was 4.6 months. These observations give the impression that monetary growth and business activity have similar cycles, and that peaks and troughs in money most often precede those in the real economy. There also is evidence,

TABLE 1-1   Timing of Business Cycle Turning Points and Turning Points in the Growth Rate of Money

(1) Economic peak	(2) Money peak	(3) Lag, months	(4) Economic trough	(5) Money trough	(6) Lag, months
Jan. 1910	Jun. 1909	−7	Jun. 1908	Feb. 1908	−4
Jan. 1913	Jun. 1912	−7	Jan. 1912	Aug. 1910	−17
Aug. 1918	Jul. 1917	−13	Dec. 1914	Dec. 1914	0
Jan. 1920	Mar. 1920	+2	Mar. 1919	May 1918	−10
May 1923	May 1923	0	Jul. 1921	Jul. 1921	0
Oct. 1926	Sep. 1925	−13	Jul. 1924	Mar. 1924	−4
Aug. 1929	Apr. 1928	−16	Nov. 1927	Dec. 1926	−11
May 1937	Jul. 1936	−10	Mar. 1933	Apr. 1933	+1
Feb. 1945	Oct. 1945	+8	Jun. 1938	May 1938	−1
Jul. 1953	Dec. 1952	−7	Oct. 1949	Jan. 1950	+3
Jul. 1957	Sep. 1955	−22	Aug. 1954	Apr. 1954	−4
May 1960	May 1959	−12	Apr. 1958	Jan. 1958	−3
			Feb. 1961	Jun. 1960	−8

which is not displayed in the table, that the severity of recessions is related to the magnitude of the decline in monetary growth. In the large majority of business cycles, when money stopped expanding, the economy eventually entered a recession. When money growth resumed, the economy later regained its upward path.

The observation that reversals of M-2 growth precede those of real output suggests a cause-and-effect relationship that the Federal Reserve can exploit for the purpose of stabilizing the economy. If the central bank can gain control over the money supply, it can prevent its growth rate from falling and perhaps forestall an untimely recession. Or, it can regulate the rate at which money grows, restraining it when inflation increases and encouraging it when unemployment becomes a problem. The lag between the change in monetary policy and its effects might be highly uncertain, but eventually the economy would move in the desired direction.

Manifestations of money's powers over business are not limited to data prior to 1960, but in recent years research methods have changed. Econometric modeling has replaced cycle dating, but the concepts involved are the same. Econometric models have become increasingly elaborate over the years as economists have reached for more specific information, but almost all models can be reduced to relatively simple expressions that relate changes in the gross national product to changes in a few variables, of which money growth is one. An early example of these reduced forms was estimated at the Federal Reserve Bank of St. Louis in 1968. It can be written as

$$\%\Delta GNP = 0.02 + 0.015\%\Delta M_t + 0.010\%\Delta(M-1) \\ + 0.008\%\Delta(M-2)\ldots \quad (1)$$

The dependent variable in this equation is the growth rate of GNP without adjustment for price inflation. The explanatory variables are the growth rate of the money supply and the rate of government expenditures on goods and services. Simply stated, the expression says that on average over the 20 years through 1967, a 1 percent increase in the growth rate of money, all else equal, adds 0.15 percent to the growth of GNP during the quarter when it occurs, 0.10 percent to the growth of GNP during the next quarter,

0.08 percent in the one after that, and so on. Or, taking the statement more literally, the growth rate of GNP during any quarter is the result of current and past growth in the money supply. The contribution of the current quarter's growth is 0.15 percent, of the previous quarter's is 0.10 percent, and so forth. Stated in this manner the econometric evidence is analogous to the cycle dating results, except that the former technique looked only at turning points in money. The statistical procedure is superior in that it can state the growth of GNP at any time as the result of a weighted average of past money growth. The implications of the two types of evidence for the Federal Reserve are approximately the same: control over the GNP can be had by regulating the growth of money.

Another body of evidence that has influenced policy thinking in the United States comes from recent studies of the causes of the Great Depression. The initial reason monetary policy fell into disuse was the belief that it had failed during the years 1930 to 1933— that the Federal Reserve had done its best to revive the economy but could not prevent the Depression. And then, after 1933, interest rates fell to 1 percent or lower, yet the economy seemed to stagnate and not respond to the incentives of cheap credit. This period more than any other is responsible for the mindless axiom, taught to millions of college sophomores, that monetary policy can only push on a string.

Within the last decade, professional opinion on the Depression has swung 180 degrees. Rather than an example of the impotence of money, the Great Depression now is seen as a demonstration of its power. The intellectual basis for this change was the realization by economists that low interest rates are neither a necessary nor a sufficient condition for stimulative monetary policy. They just as easily could signify a dormant economy, as high interest rates now are recognized to signify an inflationary one. A second look at the data from the years before 1933 reveals that the Federal Reserve did less to resist the economy's decline than once was thought. It permitted the money supply to fall by over 30 percent between the middle of 1929 and early 1933. A comparable decline today would require M-1 to contract by $600 million every week for 3½ years.

They also permitted one-fifth of the commercial banks to close their doors. A few interest rates, mostly those on Treasury securities, did come down during the period, but it is doubtful that the declines were the result of Federal Reserve activities. All of this does not say that the Federal Reserve and the monetary collapse were the only causes of the Depression. The country may well have experienced a sharp recession even if the central bank had supported the money supply, but its failure to prevent the monetary contraction had a lot to do with making the Great Depression great.

The period after 1933 has been similarly reconsidered. Shortly after the commercial banking system was restabilized by the holiday of March 1933, the money supply commenced to expand. Production and employment began to move ahead, slowly at first, but the output of goods and services increased by nearly 60 percent between mid-1933 and the beginning of 1937. The force of this advance often is overlooked because it stopped short of regaining the previous prosperity. The economy might have gone farther and carried completely out of the Depression, but the Federal Reserve raised reserve requirements in August of 1936, and business turned downward six months later.

Problems of Theory and Practice

The preceding survey has been presented in a purposely affirmative spirit without critical commentary. It would be a mistake, however, to conclude that this evidence is universally accepted or that the fundamental problems of monetary policy are solved. They are not. One doesn't have to be a confirmed monetarist to advocate money supply targeting as the basis for public policy, but it helps. Officials of the Federal Reserve are quick to say that the money supply is crucial to several versions of economic theory, and the Federal Reserve's commitment to aggregates targeting does not make it a monetarist institution. Yet, in fact, most of the support for money supply control comes from the monetarists. Economists who are trained in the Keynesian tradition will, when trapped, admit that money control is not inconsistent with a Keynesian approach to policy, but they dwell more on the failures of this method than on its achievements. Oddly enough, the monetarists are not pleased with the Federal Reserve's performance either. They perceive the central bank to be well intentioned but to have bungled because of a vestigial fixation with interest rates.

The Federal Reserve's efforts to control the economy by regulating money growth are dogged by problems of both theory and practice. There are, for example, fundamental reasons to doubt that the policy-induced changes in the growth rate of money can systematically affect economic conditions. Standard neoclassical theory implies a reasonably stable relationship between the rate at which the money supply expands and the growth rate of GNP measured in current dollars—that is without correction for inflation. However, it is ambiguous concerning the immediate division of each dollar's worth of additional GNP between more goods and higher prices. When the Federal Reserve shifts from, say, slow money growth to faster, it cannot predict whether the result will be stronger business or just more inflation. The evidence summarized in the previous section suggests that the initial effect at least is more real output, and inflation responds some time later. That is why cyclical turns in money growth correlate with turns in business conditions. When the central bank restricts the growth of money, intending to stem inflation, the economy first responds by going into recession, and the price effects come later.

In recent years, economists have become concerned with the converse of this problem. They point out that the improvement in business conditions that historically has followed an acceleration of money growth has been largely fortuitous and has occurred only because policy changes caught people by surprise, and they didn't foresee its inflationary consequences. Once the public—individuals and businesses—learn that more money eventually means faster inflation, they will respond to expansive policy not with more spending and investing but by marking up their price and wage demands. The immediate response to a shift in central bank policy will be a change in the price level but little if any change in output. The Federal Reserve, then, would be able to control prices, but they would be powerless to affect the unemployment rate or the pace of economic growth.

Perverse as this argument sounds to people who learned their economics from Professor Samuelson's textbook, there is evidence to support it. In Latin American countries, where the central banks make frequent and large changes in policy, the response of the unemployment rates to each measure of stimulus is mild. Evidently, people in these countries have become immune to swings in money growth. They see changes in official policy, they mark up their prices, and they go about their business.

A conclusion that often is drawn from these observations is that the Federal Reserve should abandon countercyclical policy. If variability in money growth is reflected mainly in variability in the inflation rate, the Federal Reserve would serve best by finding the rate of money growth that is consistent with stable prices and holding actual growth at that rate. The central bank would be relieved of any judgmental responsibility and would concern itself with the mechanical problems of keeping the money supply on the designated path. Obviously, the Federal Reserve rejects this advice and prefers to rely on the historical connection between money and income. Yet the drift of thinking both inside the Federal Reserve and outside of it is away from activist policy. Individual governors, for example, now speak as often of the limitations of the Federal Reserve's influence as of its extent, and one hears a good deal less about "fine tuning" than once was the case.

Alternative Approaches to Policy

Getting a Handle on Money

In the event the Federal Reserve ever abandons countercyclical policy and adopts a constant-growth-rate rule, its staff economists need not fear the loss of their jobs. There still would be ample work to do because the two problems that most preoccupy the Federal Reserve now would remain: (1) How does the central bank determine what is money? (2) How does it bring money under its control? In brief, the question of defining money arises because there are several assets that can serve some of the purposes of money. These assets are secure, liquid, and either can be used directly as means of payments or can be exchanged easily for a demand deposit. A list of them would include currency and demand deposits, but it also would include savings deposits, negotiable certificates of deposits, security repurchase agreements, money market funds, and credit card balances. Economic theory implies the Federal Reserve can influence prices and production by manipulating the nation's money supply, but upon which specific assets should it dwell?

The historical data indicate that M-1 (demand deposits plus currency) and M-2 are as good monies as any other aggregate, which is why the Federal Reserve uses them for monetary policy. However, much of the evidence is taken from times when the financial system in the United States was simpler than it is now, and the public had fewer alternatives to holding demand deposits and currency. As the financial system has become more specific, several other liquid assets have arisen, and these have eroded the relationship between the national income and M-1 or M-2. In 1978, for example, the dollar value of GNP was about $100 billion larger than one would have predicted from the level of M-2. This understatement occurs because M-2 is not so unique a money as it once was. People now use security repurchase agreements and thrift deposits where they once used demand and savings deposits.

The more general statement of this problem often is phrased in terms of the effects of financial innovation upon the velocity of money. Velocity is a term that is much more widely used than it is understood. In short, it is a number that relates the money supply to GNP. That is, it is the number of times the stock of money must turn over to support the level of aggregate spending:

$$GNP = MV \qquad (2)$$

or

$$V = GNP/M \qquad (3)$$

For example, if the money stock (M) is $900 billion and GNP is $2700 billion, then velocity is 3, or each dollar must turn over 3 times in the course of a year to accommodate the rate of spending. Velocity, unlike unemployment or industrial production or the money stock, cannot be directly measured; in fact, it is simply the number that makes expression (2) hold. This does not mean it is devoid of content. On the contrary, the concept of velocity embodies some very important considerations for policy makers. Velocity is not a constant, so the money managers cannot mechanically infer a GNP from the growth of money. As a minimum, they must first consider those forces in the economy that are working to alter velocity before deciding upon how fast to let money increase. And this is where financial innovation comes in. The development of better and better substitutes for M-1 and M-2 balances, in terms of higher yields with little sacrifice in liquidity, suggests that people will try to economize on such balances, but there will be no concomitant reduction in spending. In other words, it will require fewer M-1 balances to support a given level of GNP, which means that the velocity of M-1 will increase.

This is an important conclusion, for it says that financial innovation will typically increase the velocity of standard measures of money. In devising policy, then, the Federal Reserve must be cognizant of these trends, for, if it were not, it would constantly be setting growth targets for the aggregates that were too high, and policy would become an engine for inflation.

Monetary Control

Elementary textbooks in economics usually contain a demonstration of the mechanism by which bank deposits expand following an injection of bank reserves. Judging from these examples, the task of controlling the money supply is no problem at all. The Federal Reserve need only impose reserve requirements upon those financial institutions whose deposits comprise money and then adjust the amount of reserves in the system by the desired amount. The "money multiplier" process will do the rest. Unfortunately for the Federal Reserve, the world lacks the simplicity of textbooks. Funds move into and out of commercial banks, and the Federal Reserve has to exert a considerable effort just to monitor the level of bank reserves. Moreover, the public is forever altering the relationship between bank reserves and bank deposits by shifting their own funds from demand deposits to savings deposits, from deposits in Federal Reserve member banks to nonmembers, and from deposits in general into cash. The Federal Reserve cannot control these shifts and cannot predict them well. Indeed, it often doesn't learn of them until well after they have occurred.

The central bank faces another impediment to money control in the nation's preference for low and stable interest rates. When yields rise as a consequence of the Federal Reserve's efforts to reduce money growth, dark messages emanate from the White House, such as "These aren't the increases we wanted and they are not the ones we ordered," and members of Congress wonder aloud if an independent central bank best serves the public interest. Beyond these pressures, the Federal Open Market Committee is genuinely concerned with the smooth functioning of financial markets and would prefer not to let interest rates change too rapidly. But at times forces develop in the economy that would cause the money supply to rise or fall by large amounts, and to check these forces the Federal Reserve would have to allow short-term interest rates to move by a quick three or four percentage points or more. This it has been reluctant to do, and to avoid it the Federal Reserve has let the money supply go where it will.

A Better Mousetrap

Given the difficulty of running a monetary policy based on the money supply as well as the uncertainty of its results, it seems only natural to wonder if there is not a simpler, more direct, better way for the Federal Reserve to proceed. Alas, there seems not to be—at least none that is obviously superior. One suggestion that is popular among business executives is that the Federal Reserve should concentrate on the volume of credit in the economy rather than the supply of money. Credit seems closer to the essence of business, and the ease with which it can be obtained influences many business decisions. The trend of modern economics, however, is away from credit-driven theories of the business cycle. The statistical relationship between credit and economic activity is ragged, and credit seems more the result of business transactions than their cause. On more pragmatic grounds, if the Federal Reserve cannot control the money supply, why should it have any better luck with credit? Money and most of its closer substitutes emanate from three or four types of financial institutions. In the United States, there are at least a dozen different lending institutions. Indeed, every person who saves is a potential source of credit.

A more serious alternative to aggregates policy is one in which the Federal Reserve concentrates strictly upon interest rates. The proponents of this method argue that investment—especially business expenditure on plant and equipment—is the driving force of the economy, and investment is sensitive to the cost of credit. Changes in the flow of investment are said to have widespread effects upon the economy and cause GNP to rise or fall by several times the original change in investment. By altering interest rates and inducing relatively minor adjustments to expenditures on capital goods, the Federal Reserve would obtain a broad purchase on the pace of business.

Between 1952 and 1970, the Federal Reserve actually pursued a stabilization policy predicated upon interest rates and the availability of credit, but over time it moved slowly away from that approach. The change was motivated not so much by strong theoretical considerations as by the fact that managing interest rates presented more problems than controlling the money supply. Each of the problems that the Federal Reserve now encounters in the money supply has its interest rate analog. Economic theory provides no more explicit guidance in selecting an interest rate than it does in defining money. In the American financial system, there are at least 100 different interest rates. Upon which one would the Federal Reserve pin its hopes? Moreover, the proper focus of central bank attention would be real interest rates—market yields adjusted for the public's expected rate of inflation over the term of any loan. The Federal Reserve cannot measure expected inflation rates. Expectations are states of mind. They affect people's behavior but are nowhere recorded. The Federal Reserve might be able to estimate them reasonably well if the inflation rate were steady, but it isn't, and existing estimating procedures break down when the observed inflation rate fluctuates.

Measuring real interest rates is one problem; making them behave is another. The Federal Reserve's influence over market yields is strongest in the shorter maturities. By altering the supply of bank reserves, it can fairly well dictate the Federal funds rate, and, through the funds rate, it can move the commercial paper, Treasury bill, and other short-term yields. Many of the expenditures that stabilization policy would hope to alter, however, depend upon long-term rates, like mortgages and corporate bonds. The Federal Reserve would have a very limited influence over these expenditures because it has little power over longer-term interest rates. In a very general way, all interest rates rise and fall together, but the spreads between long- and short-term interest rates change frequently and by large amounts.

In the popular view, the Federal Reserve is responsible for the level of every interest rate, but the Federal Reserve's record at interest rate manipulation argues to the contrary. Consider the famous Operation Twist, a program that but for its catchy name already would be long forgotten. During the early 1960s, the central bank set out to raise short rates and lower longer ones for the expressed purpose of attracting international capital to the United States while not discouraging domestic investment. Operation Twist was an idea that originated in the Treasury, and the Federal Reserve's commitment to it was never quite clear, but the Open Market Desk did make itself for some time a buyer of Treasury bonds and a seller of bills. The amount by which these operations twisted the yield curve is imperceptible to the naked eye. Investors would not accept lower yields on bonds. As the Federal Reserve bought, they sold. When the Federal Reserve sold bills, they bought, and so it went. The public's evaluation of securities of different maturity was determined by fundamental economic factors. Against these factors, the Federal Reserve could not prevail.

Operation Twist is not an isolated example. One could cite similar incidents, but they all would illustrate essentially the same point: Managing interest rates is at least as difficult as managing the money supply, and in choosing to base its policies on the money supply, the Federal Reserve is not overlooking an obviously preferable alternative. The methods and achievements of monetary policy are under continuous review, both within the Federal Reserve and by university economists. One can envision a time when the Federal Reserve will discover a better method of economic stabilization and switch to it. That would be in the future. For now money supply targeting is the game. This being the case, it imposes several requirements upon the daily operations of the central bank, which in turn affect bank reserves and interest rates. These operating practices and interest rates relationships are the subject matter of the remainder of this book.

Open Market Operations and the Federal Funds Rate

Introduction

From some time in the middle of 1970 until September of 1979, the Federal Reserve tried to regulate the growth of money by changing the levels of short-term interest rates. When money grew too fast, it raised short-term rates; when money grew too slowly, it lowered them. Using the Federal funds rate as its guide, the Open Market Desk decided where it wanted short rates and then provided the banking system with whatever reserves it needed to hold rates in place. Then, in October 1979, the Federal Reserve announced it no longer would peg the Federal funds rate. Instead it would guide open market operations by the growth of reserves in the banking system and let market forces determine the level of the Federal funds and other short-term interest yields. At the same time, the Board of Governors imposed an 8 percent reserve requirement on some of the Federal funds that member banks borrow from lenders outside of the Federal Reserve System. These changes had two immediate effects on the debt markets and then a third that revealed itself a short time later. First, a two-tier market in Federal funds has developed in which lenders from outside the Federal Reserve System receive a rate that is 92 percent of the rate that prevails in trades between member institutions. If the rate in the member market is 10 percent, outsiders receive 9.2 percent. Second, the Federal funds rate itself, the one received by both members and nonmembers, has become subject to wider day-to-day and weekly fluctuations. Where its normal trading range formerly was ¼ percent, it now moves by as much as 2 percent in a single day. The third effect, which first appeared at the onset of recession in April 1979, is that the funds rate is more flexible over the course of a business cycle. It need not rise to higher peaks or fall to lower troughs, but since it is more responsive to the demand for bank reserves, it rises faster when the demand for bank credit grows and falls faster when that demand recedes.

This chapter describes and analyzes the market for Federal funds and the related market for security repurchase agreements. It will discuss the interactions by which the Federal funds rate is determined under the new system, in which the Federal Reserve targets bank reserves, and under the old, in which the Open Market Desk fixed the funds rate directly. It would be unwise to disregard the former system too quickly. The Federal Reserve has tried reserve targeting before only to restore the Federal funds rate peg, and it could well do so again. The difference between the old and new methods is, in fact, quite small because both are dominated by the consequences of lagged reserve accounting. Under lagged accounting, the reserves that Federal Reserve member banks must hold during any statement week are determined by their average liabilities during the week ending two weeks prior. This regulation imposes operating requirements upon the Open Market Desk that limit its activities regardless of whether it seeks to manage the growth of bank reserves or to stipulate a Federal funds rate.

The World from the Funds Desk

Each week, banks that are members of the Federal Reserve System must hold reserves against their deposits and other reservable liabilities. The reserve requirements range from 2 percent against long-term certificates of deposit to 16 percent against demand deposits (see Table 2-1), and can be held as either cash in the banks' vaults or deposits at a Federal Reserve Bank. Requirements must be satisfied on average throughout each week, so the excess reserves of one day can be balanced against the deficiency of another.

Most of the Federal Reserve's 5000 member banks regard these reserves as a burden thrust upon them by someone from Washing-

TABLE 2-1 Member Bank Reserve Requirements

Type of deposit and deposit intervals	Percent
Net demand deposits	
First $2 million	7
$2–$10 million	9½
$10–$100 million	11¾
$100–$400 million	12¾
Over $400 million	16¼
Time and savings deposits	
Savings	3
Time—first $5 million	
30–179-day maturity	3
180 days to 4 years	2½
Over 4 years	1
Time—over $5 million	
30–179-day maturity	6
180 days to 4 years	2½
Over 4 years	1
Managed liabilities in excess of $100 million	8

ton who never made a loan. Each week, they compute their requirements and tally them against the eligible assets on hand. Most of any excess cash they might have is deposited with a larger correspondent bank, or, if they fall short, the same correspondent usually provides what they need. The large majority of banks go no farther. They return to making mortgages and automobile loans and bother with their liquidity position only if it intrudes. In contrast to these, a small minority of institutions—possibly the 100 largest—do much more. They treat liquidity as they would any other asset—an opportunity to trade for profit. Each week, they move hundreds of millions of dollars, "buying" when they perceive the rate on overnight loans is too low and "selling" when it seems high. Their funds traders struggle to stay abreast of their reserve requirements, and somehow along the way they manage to meet them. The good ones rarely miss by more than a few dollars.

The market in which these banks exchange short-term loans is called the Federal funds market. The name derives from Federal Reserve funds, because originally such transactions led to an immediate change in the ownership of deposits at a Federal Reserve Bank. Most of them still do. Federal funds loans are settled in immediately available funds that are transferred between lender and borrower over the Federal Reserve wire—a high-speed communications system between large commercial banks and the 12 district Federal Reserve Banks. The lender sends instructions to debit its deposit and credit that of the borrower. As a result, loans for as short a time as one day are feasible and, in fact, comprise the majority of transactions. Since ownership of deposits at Federal Reserve Banks is exchanged, the Federal funds market is the natural place for a bank to look when it needs reserves, and in earlier days reserve adjustment motivated most Federal funds transactions. Since 1968, however, many banks consider the Federal funds market a source of general funding and borrow there much as they would in the markets for certificates of deposit or Eurodollars. The main differences are in the term of loan and in reserve requirements.

All of the large borrowers of Federal funds are commercial banks, but many active lenders are not. Even though they do not hold deposits at Federal Reserve Banks, banks outside the Federal Reserve System, agencies of the United States government, branches of foreign commercial banks, Edge Act corporations, and foreign central banks can participate in the Federal funds trading. Until October 1979, Federal Reserve Regulation D exempted their Federal funds loans to member banks from reserve requirements. Now a Federal Reserve member who borrows these funds may have to hold an 8 percent reserve against them. With or without the requirement, the borrower receives an immediate credit to its account at the Federal Reserve Bank, just as if it had borrowed the funds from another member bank. The nonbank participants have provided increasing sums over the years, and by 1978 they accounted for about half the loans. The other half were supplied by the group of smaller commercial banks. (See Table 2-2.)

The Market for Repurchase Agreements

Like Federal funds, repurchase agreements are a form of short-term loan. The two differ in that a Federal funds loan is unsecured; but in a repurchase agreement, the borrower sells the lender a Treasury or Agency security and agrees to buy it back on a designated date at a prearranged price. The difference between the purchase and

TABLE 2-2   Lenders in the Federal Funds Market

	Percent of funds lent
Federal Reserve member banks	49.9
Domestic nonmember banks	15.4
U.S. branches of foreign banks	6.1
Edge Act corporations	0.6
Other depository institutions	16.6
All others	11.4

the repurchase prices provides the lender its income. The securities are collateral for the loan, and the lender either takes possession or receives a nonnegotiable safekeeping receipt stating that the securities are held at a Federal Reserve Bank or in the vaults of the borrowing bank.

Commercial banks are the largest borrowers of repurchase agreements, followed by dealers in government securities, who use repurchase agreements (RP) whenever they can to finance their inventories. For commercial banks, a repurchase agreement is perfectly analogous to a Federal funds loan, except it involves the work of providing collateral. For this effort, the borrower is rewarded with a lower interest rate, since the lender has the government security. Most of the time, the rate on RP is between 25 and 100 basis points below the Federal funds rate (see Figure 2-1), but the spread becomes considerably wider during times of economic stress, when the stability of some banks comes into question. In extreme conditions, as in the spring of 1974 after the collapse of Franklin National Bank, lenders have been willing to forego nearly three percentage points in interest for the safety of the government or agency collateral.

The pattern of borrowing and lending in RP is similar to that in Federal funds—the 46 largest commercial banks take in more than half the funds lent under RP, and smaller banks and thrift institutions are net providers. One important difference is that corporations, who cannot participate in Federal funds trading, are very active lenders in RP. At the end of 1977, of the $22 billion borrowed by large banks, over $10 billion came from nonfinancial corporations. (See Table 2-3.) For businesses, the RP is nearly the equivalent of an interest-bearing demand deposit. Firms with well-orga-

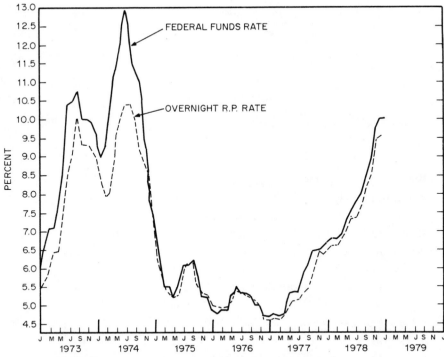

FIGURE 2-1   The rates on Federal funds and repurchase agreements rise and fall together.

nized cash management systems have a reasonably good idea each morning of the cash payments they will have to make during the day. They can place that amount in demand deposits and keep a safety margin in RP, to which they have access within one day. Another group of large lenders are state and local governments, who regularly buy between 15 percent and 20 percent of the RP

TABLE 2-3   Buyers of Repurchase Agreements— December 1977

	Percent of total
Businesses	54.9
Federal Reserve member banks	12.6
State and local governments	17.1
Securities dealers	8.9
All others	6.5

sold by banks and at least that much of the agreements sold by securities dealers. Governments are attracted to RP for the same reason that draws corporations—substantial amounts of income from otherwise idle cash. Their liquidity management problem differs from that of corporations, however, in that it is dominated by the seasonality of tax receipts.

Most repurchase agreements last only one day, and even lenders who plan to remain in RP for an extended period usually renegotiate each day and receive the then current rate of return. Lenders who want to lock up a rate can make agreements lasting anywhere between two days and a year. These longer agreements, called term RP, comprise about 25 percent of the market. They usually pay a rate of return that is above the overnight rate as well as above the yield on Treasury bills of similar maturity. Lenders demand more for the RP than for the bill because their funds are tied up for a stipulated period of time, whereas they always can get out of the bill by selling it.

Federal Funds and Liability Management

Bank treasurers face several potential sources of funding, of which Federal funds are the most liquid and sometimes the lowest in cost. Other forms of borrowing like certificates of deposit, commercial paper, notes, or bonds usually bear a higher interest rate, but they are of longer maturity and so do not have to be refunded as frequently. The longer-term markets also are less liquid, and borrowers usually cannot borrow large amounts as quickly as they can in Federal funds. The choice among the alternative sources is a portfolio decision. By altering the liability composition of their borrowings, treasurers can obtain the combination of price, term, and risk exposure that suit their circumstances and outlook.

Aggressive commercial banks are never completely out of the Federal funds market. They always borrow something, but it is a matter of degree. During the past ten years, large banks have relied increasingly on Federal funds as a source of finance. Their Federal funds liabilities have risen both in absolute amount and as a share of their total liabilities (see Figure 2-2), although the rise in relative

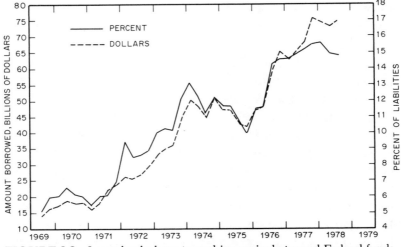

FIGURE 2-2   Large banks have turned increasingly toward Federal funds.

importance has been much less smooth than the absolute gain. Both the secular trend toward Federal funds and the cyclical deviations from trend reflect the portfolio decisions of bank treasurers. The first is a result of long-term financial planning. The persistent rise in interest rates since 1965 has provided a strong incentive for banks to lure customers out of instruments that have reserve requirements, and into repurchase agreements and Federal funds, which until recently had none. The banks have been aided in this effort by the development of on-line cash management systems, which have lowered the cost of managing overnight loans. So over time banks have been able to offer depositors an alternative that is as liquid as a demand deposit but one that pays interest as well.

A good part of the cyclical demand for Federal funds is the result of plain interest speculation by banks. Since Federal funds are at the extreme short end of the maturity spectrum, their price relative to other borrowing sources goes through extraordinary fluctuations during a business cycle. For example, Table 2-4 shows the interest rates paid by top grade borrowers for loans lasting between one day and 20 years at two points during the last business cycle. Even compared to six-month certificates of deposit, the Federal funds rate went from a borrower's advantage of 85 basis points in December of 1971, to a disadvantage of 85 basis points in July 1974.

TABLE 2-4 Interest Rates at Extreme Points of a Business Cycle

	Trough—December 1971	Peak—July 1974
Federal funds	3.20	12.90
6-mo CD	4.05	12.05
7- to 10-yr aggregate bonds	6.60	9.50
20-yr aggregate bonds	7.20	10.20

When commercial banks sense a move toward monetary restraint by the Federal Reserve, they attempt to lengthen their liabilities. Anticipating sustained rises in the Federal funds rate, banks that are able to do so go from borrowing overnight to issuing six-month and one-year certificates of deposit, longer-term time deposits, and even long-term bonds. The objective is to lock up current borrowing costs and avoid even higher ones as monetary policy becomes more restrictive. These shifts to longer-dated instruments put the borrowers at risk. Those who lengthen their debt early, before the term structure of interest rates becomes inverted, have to pay a premium to extend because longer-term rates still exceed the overnight rates. In effect, they are betting that they have seen something in monetary policy that the general market has not and that the Federal funds rate will rise faster than others anticipate. They pay more now but expect future savings that will more than compensate them. Miscalculations can be very expensive, however, because banks that extend too soon have their borrowing costs increase in a way that cannot be recouped in higher lending rates. Still, bank treasurers have become increasingly prone to making an early bet and extending, because interest rates during each of the last three cycles exceeded the public's initial expectation. Treasurers who avoided paying those astronomical rates were heroes among their peers and probably now hold bigger jobs.

Despite the obvious incentives to avoid Federal funds during the late stages of an interest rate cycle, Figure 2-2 shows that at the peak of the last cycle banks used Federal funds more than ever. Bankers probably were as surprised as everyone else that interest rates got as high in 1974 as they did. Once the Federal funds rate rose beyond the level that people had projected would be the top, there was a tendency to see each new level as the peak rate. So banks that would have extended at an earlier stage actually did the reverse. If rates were at the peak, the smart move was to borrow short and extend later when rates fell. The obvious danger in that strategy was that rates pushed still higher, and borrowers who got into this box ended by paying the highest rates throughout the peak period.

Probably the most common reason why banks move into and out of the Federal funds market is unpredictable changes in loan demand. Aside from ordinary daily and weekly fluctuations, when financial markets come under stress banks do an increasing share of the business lending. Marginal business firms, who can place their commercial paper during ordinary times, are closed out during periods of high interest rates and economic uncertainty, and they look to their banks for loans. Even top grade firms borrow for shorter periods when rates are high, and commercial banks get a share of that incremental demand. The banks, of course, recognize that this demand is temporary but have difficulty predicting its exact duration. Since most of these loans are priced with floating rates—a specified margin over the prime rate—banks can accommodate their customers and avoid risk by funding them with Federal funds.

The Suppliers of Federal Funds

The 100 largest commercial banks are nearly always net borrowers of Federal funds, and the smaller 10,000 are always lenders. The reasons behind this division are much the same as those which explain why large businesses maintain relatively smaller cash positions than do smaller firms. They do not need cash any less, but they deal in amounts of sufficient size to justify paying a good salary to someone who will know how to get cash only when they need it. They substitute management and personnel for cash balances. Large commercial banks are organized in such a way that each department head knows the current cost of funds and can act as if he or she had unlimited call on money at that rate. The department head's job is to scan the markets for lending opportunities that offer rates of return above the borrowing cost—if not in business lending then in government securities, acceptances, or even the liabilities of other banks. It is someone else's job to worry about the bank's solvency.

Smaller banks may be run by equally aggressive people, but vigilance costs money, and they simply do not move enough funds to pay for close management. Once they have exhausted the opportunities in their local lending markets, these banks are left with idle cash, and the Federal funds market is the ideal place to put it. Federal funds provide a market rate of return, they are liquid, and once a relationship is set up with a broker or an accommodating bank, participation in the market is nearly costless. Lenders simply check the rates and transfer their funds over the Fed wire. If a bank is lending to a larger correspondent bank, it need not do even that because chances are its funds already are on deposit with the correspondent.

Like the borrowers, the lending banks also have a portfolio problem. Their opportunities are not restricted to only commercial lending and Federal funds, and just as the large banks do not always borrow in funds, the more modest institutions also invest elsewhere. However, the tendency is for these banks to keep a large share of their assets in Federal funds because of the liquidity funds offer, and it takes sizable rate spreads to draw them into less liquid investments. Then, too, the transactions cost of buying longer-term investments generally exceed those of selling Federal funds. That is why several very small banks make Federal funds their principal source of income. During periods when the yield curve is inverted, about four years in the last ten, the Federal funds rate is among the best yields around and the lending institutions earn enormous spreads over their deposit costs. This explains why little-known banks so often report historically high earnings when the rest of the economy is in difficult financial straits.

Relationships in the Federal funds market between borrowers and lenders grew originally out of the network of correspondent banks. Until the mid-1960s, banks that did not have the personnel to manage a portfolio of Treasury bills and bankers acceptances kept their liquid balances in nonearning deposits at other banks. This practice presented no problems when short-term interest rates were 1 percent or 2 percent. But once inflation worked itself into market rates and raised them above purely nominal levels, nonearning deposits became an expensive luxury, and pressure increased to revamp the correspondent banking system. The Comptroller of the Currency first responded to the pressure in 1964 by declaring that Federal funds transactions are not loans but sales, and supplying institutions are not restricted by regulations that limit loans to any single borrower to 10 percent of the lender's capital. The Federal Reserve Board took complementary action by ruling that member banks could buy the correspondent balances of nonmembers as Federal funds, which effectively removed reserve requirements from such deposits and brought nonmember banks into the Federal funds market. These two regulation changes assured that commercial banks away from the nation's financial centers could earn a current yield on their idle funds, but they are not themselves responsible for the growth of Federal funds trading. That had to wait for the introduction of lagged reserve accounting. After 1968, when the money center banks were freed from the constraint of having to maintain reserves on their current liabilities, they began to compete for funds from every available source, and trading volume in Federal funds increased by 400 percent in less than two years.

The simplicity of the Federal funds market was upset in late 1979, when the Board of Governors imposed an 8 percent marginal reserve requirement on the managed liabilities of member banks. They included in managed liabilities such items as large certificates of deposit, loans from foreign branches, and Federal funds and repurchase agreements with lenders from outside of the Federal Reserve System. The reserve requirement is applied to the excess of the sum of these liabilities over their outstanding amounts during the last two weeks of September 1979. As a result, banks that are over their base amounts must hold an 8 percent reserve against Federal funds purchased from nonmembers. Such loans are now more expensive to the Federal Reserve member banks than the same loan from another member, and members will accept funds from nonmembers only at a discount from the rate they would have to pay another member. During periods when the majority of member banks are over their bases, the Federal funds market divides into two tiers, with nonmembers receiving a rate that is, on average, 92 percent of whatever rate prevails among members.

Federal Funds and Financial Efficiency

The development of the Federal funds market has had a number of implications for the process of saving and investment in the American economy. For one, it unifies the banking system by giving all banks the same opportunity cost of funds against which to measure their local opportunities. Hence, it increases the efficiency of investment by assuring that all calls for funds from commercial banks are judged against a uniform standard. In effect, the Federal funds market transforms the collection of some 14,000 individually owned banks into something like a few large banks with thousands of branches. Each "branch" collects deposits and serves the local loan market, making all loans with a prospective rate of return above the likely Federal funds rate. The monies not employed locally are sent to the "home office" by way of the Federal funds market, from which they are distributed to branches that can profitably invest more than they attract in deposits. Each branch earns the spread between the Federal funds rate and the rates it pays on deposits. Income earned from this spread has to cover the cost of operating the branch, provide a yield on the capital it ties up, and also return some rent on the monopoly that was acquired with the purchase of the state of Federal bank charter.

Setting the Federal Funds Rate

Most of the time, the Federal funds rate trades in the general vicinity of the rates on 90-day certificates of deposits, bankers acceptances, short-term Treasury bills, and the Federal Reserve discount rate (see Figure 2-3). It usually is below the rates on money market instruments and above the discount rate, but it falls below even the discount rate during periods of monetary ease. The proximate reason why the funds rate and other short-term rates move so closely is that many investors use the Federal funds rate as their opportunity cost of capital. It is a rate they can earn easily and with little risk by placing funds in the overnight market. Investors usually require some yield premium—called positive carry—in order to

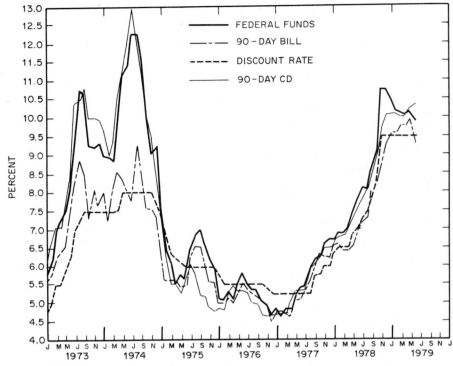

FIGURE 2-3   Short-term interest rates.

draw them out of Federal funds and into longer-dated instruments. Short-term Treasury bills are an exception to this rule because they are a favorite of foreign central banks, who place a particularly high value upon liquidity, but it is generally the case with other investments. Whenever the Federal funds rate rises and eliminates carry, investors sell their money market investments and refrain from buying new issues until the market reestablishes the spreads they require, a process that normally takes somewhere between a few minutes and a couple of days. The converse is equally true when the funds rate falls. A more fundamental explanation for the proximity of rates on Federal funds and money market instruments is that as investments they offer approximately the same properties— very liquid, low risk, taxable income. In a free market, one would expect the income streams from essentially identical investments to bear the same rates of discount.

In those frequent instances when spreads of any size do develop, as happened in the summer of 1974 when the funds rate was 3 percent higher than the certificate of deposits (CD) rate, it is usually because the Federal funds rate is for overnight and the others are for 90 days or longer. In comparing Federal funds against other investments, money managers have to consider the prospective average yield on funds over the life of the longer investment. When they anticipate a decline in the funds rate, they attempt to secure high yields on longer-term investments, and their demands drive down longer rates relative to the yield on spot funds. The flux of yield spreads is pushed from the supply side as well. When commercial banks, for example, foresee higher funds rates, they try to lengthen the term of their liabilities by selling certificates of deposits. The CD market becomes crowded with new issues at a time when investors are turning reluctant about tying up their capital, and CD rates can rise quickly. They would go up in any case by virtue of the change in the public's expectations about the future of the Federal funds rate, but the large new issues speed the process and, at times, cause an overadjustment. When rates overreact, it is the job of good money market traders to play the role of speculators by bringing the high-yielding certificates into inventory and thus bid their rates back to more realistic levels.

The Federal funds rate itself is most immediately determined by demand and supply in that market. Previous sections of this chapter have summarized the several factors that influence the demand and supply of Federal funds, and these factors play themselves out in the daily push and shove of the market. Briefly, what happens is that large commercial banks have an incentive to borrow Federal funds so long as they can identify investments with likely yields in excess of the funds rate. Their bidding for funds raises the rate and attracts into the market cash that might have remained idle or have been placed elsewhere. In the absence of Federal Reserve intervention, this bidding continues, and the volume of transactions grows until the amounts of funds that borrowers want to take out of the market match the amounts lenders bring to it. The Federal funds rate is then in equilibrium for that day. The bidding recommences the next day, and a new rate is established.

The Role of Bank Reserves

The analysis of the sources and uses of Federal funds in the introductory portions of this chapter stressed that reserve management is but one of several employments for Federal funds. Nevertheless, the basis for the Federal Reserve's power over the Federal funds rate is its ability to alter the amount of reserves in the banking system and the composition of reserves between those supplied in the open market and those provided by rediscounting. All financial markets are affected to some degree by changes in bank reserves, but the impact is most direct and most quickly seen in Federal funds. The truth could not be otherwise because regardless of the way in which the proceeds ultimately are used, the Federal funds market is the market for deposits at Federal Reserve Banks, and the balance of supply and demand is altered immediately by changes in the total of these deposits.

Sales of Federal funds do not necessarily involve a transfer of reserves between banks, but in fact most do. Even when the seller is not a Federal Reserve member, or not a bank at all, the lending of funds overnight gives the borrower a claim on the lender's demand deposit that must be cleared immediately at the regional Federal Reserve Bank. Thus, reserves change hands. When a member bank buys as Federal funds the balance of the correspondent bank, reserves do not change hands if the purchaser is simply paying for funds it already holds as a correspondent deposit. The member is preventing a reserve shift that would take place if the correspondent would otherwise move its deposits to another bank.

These facts have certain consequences for the operation of the Federal funds market, which can be seen with the following example. Consider a day in which the banking system has $100 million of excess reserves, and two particular banks, say Chase Manhattan and Citibank, begin the day with exactly zero excess. Assume that Citibank wants to make a loan and raises the funds by buying Federal funds from a third bank that has some surplus. The Citibank client receives a demand deposit and either spends it or directly moves it to Chase. The check clears immediately, so Chase now has equal amounts of both additional deposits and reserves. But because of lagged reserve accounting, Chase has no additional required reserves for the current statement week. The Federal funds loans of the entire banking system are up by the amount of the Citibank purchase, the banking system still has $100 million in excess reserves, and Chase now has some funds which it can hold or sell in the Federal funds market. Its decision will depend on several factors. One of these is the projection that Chase's Federal funds management has for market conditions later in the statement week. If Chase expects the funds rate to remain steady, it would be likely to keep excess reserves as close to zero as possible because it does not want to give up income, and if it unexpectedly loses reserves later on, it can always borrow them at something like the current rate. If Chase expects the Federal funds rate to move upward, it might welcome the excess as a means of raising its average reserve holdings now in order to free funds to be lent when the rate is higher. If Chase is uncertain, chances are it will hold a small reserve surplus, just as a precaution.

The decision will hinge also on the amount of discounts Chase has outstanding at the Federal Reserve Bank of New York. Banks that appear too frequently at the discount window get asked a number of questions that are a bother to answer. Rather than have the Federal Reserve poking into their affairs, banks generally prefer to conserve on discounts whenever possible. Against this, a positive interest spread between the Federal funds and discount rates is an incentive to get away with as much borrowing as possible, because a bank loses income by repaying a discount at 10 percent with cash it could sell in Federal funds at 12 percent. So Chase's funds manager would be quicker to relend the excess cash if Chase has no discounts outstanding and has not been to the window recently. The bank then would be assured that if it ran short of reserves late in the week, the window would be open to it with no questions asked.

Assume for now that Chase sells the excess. Federal funds loans rise further, and some other bank then has more reserves, which it, in turn can relend. In fact, it matters very little what Chase does with its excess reserves, so long as it does not keep them idle. If it retired a certificate of deposit, the reserves would move to another bank, which could place them in Federal funds. The same would be true if it bought a Treasury bill. The essential point is that so long as banks have reserves they do not want to hold or to use for retiring discounts, these reserves can travel from bank to bank, generating an infinite amount of Federal funds sales. What is more, the expansion of those transactions need not raise the Federal funds rate by much so long as the reserves remain within the network of banks actively in the Federal funds market. The rate would tend upward if transactions shift funds toward banks that hold them in cash, either because they want excess reserve or because they are uncomfortable with their debts at the discount window.

As a final but important demonstration of the Federal funds market, consider a week in which the total of reserves supplied by the Open Market Desk plus the outstanding discounts leaves member banks with insufficient amounts to meet their requirements. The banks would be unable to reduce their reserve needs because requirements stem from liabilities of two weeks past and are beyond changing. Members would have no alternative but to try to borrow reserves from one another or go to the discount window. Of course, no individual bank would know that the system as a whole had a reserve deficit, and each time one of them succeeded in drawing a dollar, it would increase the shortage of another by that amount. Instead of there being a very elastic supply of Federal funds loans, funds would be exceedingly difficult to borrow, and the rate would be bid quickly to quite high levels. As the rate rose, its spread over the discount rate would increase, and more banks would overcome their reluctance and borrow at the window. The additional reserves would increase the supply of Federal funds, lower the demand, and the rate would regain its equilibrium—but at a level higher than at the start of the week.

Open Market Operations

The Federal Open Market Committee provides the Desk with a series of weekly reserve targets that are consistent with the Committee's long-term objectives for reserve growth. The Manager for Domestic Operations tries to guide actual bank reserves along this path, in the knowledge that he will miss the mark during many individual weeks, but might be close on average during periods of a month or so. Because of lagged reserve accounting, the amount of reserves that will be held by the banking system is predetermined at the beginning of each week by the members' requirements. The manager can decide only what portion he will supply and what portion he will cause banks to borrow at the discount window. As a rule, when reserve growth in the recent past has exceeded the Federal Reserve's targets, the manager provides fewer reserves and forces more borrowing. When reserve growth is below the target path, he supplies reserves more generously and allows banks to repay their discounts.

Depending upon where bank reserves stand relative to target, the manager begins each week with an objective for borrowed reserves. He has an implicit target for nonborrowed reserves as well, since the sum of borrowed and nonborrowed must equal a known quantity of required reserves plus a small margin of excess reserves. The Desk staff economists forecast the nonborrowed reserves that will be provided each week by external factors, like Federal Reserve float, and based upon these projections and his goals for nonborrowed reserves the manager decides the amounts of repurchase or matched-sale agreements the Desk will perform each day.

As most college sophomores know, when the Federal Reserve buys securities, bank reserves increase, and when it sells securities, reserves diminish. The overwhelming majority of open market operations involve either Treasury securities, government agency issues, or bankers acceptances—which the Federal Reserve buys through 34 registered dealers. Once the manager decides upon the size and duration of the agreements he wants to make, the transactions are performed quickly over direct telephone lines. Most open market operations are reversed within seven days, and during the initial call—or go-round—the dealers are asked to submit bids or offers, depending upon whether the operation is adding or draining reserves. The Desk accepts these propositions, beginning with the most competitive and working down until its order is filled. When the Federal Reserve is making repurchase agreements involving large amounts of securities, it explicitly announces that it will accept "dealer and customer collateral," meaning it will temporarily buy securities owned by both the registered securities dealers and by their customers. The Federal Reserve must take physical possession of the securities it buys. This presents no problem for Treasury bills, which have no certificates but are mere book entries at the Treasury and can be exchanged by having a computer move serial numbers from one column to another. Treasury notes or bonds have to be transported to a Federal Reserve Bank, and investors who want to participate in this market regularly keep securities with their dealers to facilitate the exchange.

Open Market Operations and the Federal Funds Rate

Open market operations often affect the Federal funds market within minutes. The first participants to feel their consequences usually are the thrift institutions, government agencies, and other nonbank operators in the market for repurchase agreements. Many of them own government securities, which they are willing to finance through repurchase agreements. If the Federal Reserve takes their securities, they are left with cash, which they relend in the Federal funds market. When the Federal Reserve's payments enter the banking system, which they do in a matter of hours, bank reserves rise. The converse takes place when the Federal Reserve sells securities under matched sale-purchase agreements. Private investors who would have had cash to lend in Federal funds or RP buy the Federal Reserve's securities, and reserves pass out of the banking system.

Open market operations also have secondary repercussions through the government securities dealers. As part of their inventory financing, dealers take loans from commercial banks. When the Federal Reserve buys their securities, the dealers have cash with which to pay down their loans. The commercial banks receive cash, which alters their Federal funds trading strategy immediately, since most banks manage their dealer loans directly from the Federal funds desk. Of course, only dealer transactions with the Federal Reserve have any effect upon the Federal funds rate. Dealers also do repurchase agreements with corporations and individuals, which might cause them to repay some dealer loans. But these transactions only move funds from one bank to another. They do not alter bank reserves or reduce the demand for private financing.

Open market operations have their greatest impact on the Federal funds rate through their influence upon bank reserves. When the manager of the domestic account decides to reduce the borrowings of member banks, he accomplishes it by providing larger amounts of reserves through the market. When the payments clear, member banks find that with their then outstanding discounts they have more reserve deposits than they need. Those banks that are uncomfortable with their borrowings can use whatever excess they have to repay their debts to the Federal Reserve. Other banks, either without discounts or unconcerned about them, will increase their offerings of Federal funds. As the funds rate comes down, more banks will find it no longer pays to remain in debt to the Federal Reserve, and member discounts will decline farther. As the borrowing level falls, excess reserves are reduced, the funds rate stops coming down, and a new equilibrium is established at a borrowings level that fulfills the Desk's intentions. If members are slow to give up their borrowed reserves, the manager can supply a few more nonborrowed reserves, drive the funds rate down another notch, and coax additional banks out of the window. In most instances, by the time the statement week ends, the excess reserves left on the books are close to zero because the banking system will have moved both the funds rate and the amount of borrowed reserves down until all redundant cash has been eliminated. This observation does not negate the fact that it was the initial perception of excess liquidity that started the process moving. If the Manager changed his mind the next week and raised his objectives for borrowed reserves, he would reverse the process by doing matched sale-purchase agreements. Banks would find themselves chronically short of reserves, bid harder for Federal funds, and increase their indebtedness to the Federal Reserve.

The ability of the Desk to control borrowed reserves and, through them, to manipulate the Federal funds rate depends crucially upon the reluctance of member banks to borrow. If members were completely and honestly indifferent to whether their reserves were borrowed or nonborrowed, whenever the funds rate exceeded the discount rate they would obtain 100 percent of their needs from the window, and the Desk would be unable to hold the Federal funds rate above the discount rate. It could keep the funds rate below the discount rate, but only by keeping borrowed reserves at zero. Fortunately for the Federal Reserve, it can ensure that banks are not indifferent to nonborrowed reserves. By requiring successively larger amounts of documentation and by keeping members aware that rediscounting is a privilege that can be refused, the Federal Reserve can maintain the distinction which the Open Market Desk uses to its advantage.

The Funds Rate Pegged

For several years before October of 1979, the Desk performed open market operations to target the Federal funds rate rather than a level of bank reserves. In each directive from the Federal Open Market Committee, the Open Market Manager received instructions on where to set the weekly average rates on Federal funds. The manager pursued these instructions by establishing strike points, usually ⅛ of a percent above and below his weekly average target. He added reserves to the banking system when the Federal funds rate reached the upper boundary and removed them when it fell toward the lower limit. As a result, borrowers of funds rarely would pay a rate above their perception of the upper intervention level, and lenders were reluctant to accept less than the lower strike rate. In effect, the action of the Open Market Desk truncated the normal supply and demand schedules, so they looked like Figure 2-4. Ordinary trading took place along the sloping portions of the curves. But if something occurred that shocked the market and caused demand to increase, the Federal Reserve would provide all that the market demanded at the higher boundary rate. If demand collapsed, the Federal Reserve would, in effect, buy whatever funds the market wanted to sell at the lower limit. This is the essence of price fixing. When market conditions were such as to force the Federal funds rate upward, trading would continue at the upper intervention point but not push through it because market participants

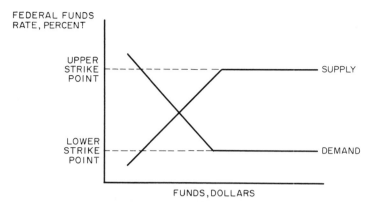

FIGURE 2-4   Supply and demand in a pegged market.

expected a move from the Desk. If the Federal Reserve remained out of the market, participants would suspect a change in the target, and the rate eventually would rise through the ceiling. A new equilibrium then would be established, either as the outcome of natural market forces or because of some later action by the Open Market Desk.

Open Market Signals

In manipulating the Federal funds rate, the Open Market Manager constantly has to cope with the problem of imperfect information. The manager usually does not know the exact amount of reserves in the banking system. He or she obviously knows whether in some general sense reserves are sufficient to meet requirements, but the margin of sufficiency is often unclear. And then, the Federal funds market does not always respond in a consistent manner to a given reserve surplus. The frictional level of excess reserves increases when reserves move to banks that do not manage their liquidity and so do not relend their unused cash. The Federal funds market can become tight even though reserves in the aggregate appear abundant.

The Desk learned to deal with imperfect information and fickle markets by relying on an informal signaling system that advised funds traders of the approved range for the Federal funds rate. The signals were open market repurchase agreements when the Federal funds rate rose ⅛ percent above target and matched sales when it fell ⅛ percent below. These signals imposed an order on the market that was, to a degree, independent of supply and demand conditions. When the Federal funds rate began to trade on either border of the usual range, market players, waiting for the Desk, did not force a market clearing at every moment. When the Desk wanted to signal a new funds rate trading range, it conveyed its intention to the market in one of a few ways. Depending upon whether the move was up or down, it either drained reserves at a funds rate where it previously added or added where it formerly drained. This was a strong direct signal, which the market understood quickly. Upon occasion, the manager may have been leaning toward, say a higher rate but wanted to see one more week's money supply figures before deciding. If the week was one in which seasonal conditions required adding reserves, that could be done by performing four-day repurchase agreements on Thursday or over the weekend on Friday. These measures added temporary reserves and kept the funds rate in its normal range. On Monday, when the reserves they provided left the system, the funds rate would tend toward a higher level because of the reserve decline. The manager then had the market set up so that if he saw the first estimate of the week's money supply and decided not to raise the funds rate, he could renew the repurchase agreements at the usual intervention point. If he decided to go to a new funds rate level, he did nothing. When the rate hit the old intervention point and the Desk did not respond, Federal funds traders quickly grasped the Desk's intent and moved the rate to higher grounds. If they did not, the Manager made the message clearer by doing overnight matched sales.

Like many complicated systems, the one used by the Federal Reserve sounds neater on paper than it was in practice. The Desk did not always do repurchase agreements at ⅛ percent above its target. Sometimes it kept the funds rate on a short leash and operated at a 1/16 percent margin. Other times the manager let funds trade on the high or low side for a day to compensate for previous aberrations hoping to bring the weekly average rate in on target. (Open Market Committee instructions were phrased in terms of weekly averages.) Or the manager might have believed a high Federal funds rate was only temporary because of a self-correcting drop in reserves. Or the manager might have felt that reserves were plentiful and that adding to them would have risked a collapse in the Federal funds rate at a later time. There always were any number of extenuating circumstances that could force the Federal funds trading away from its normal routine. When these events occurred and the Desk did not provide the expected signal, the bond and money markets became uneasy. There invariably were some people who were convinced the Federal funds rate was headed into new territory. They spread their conviction to other traders, either through the Wall Street telephone network or by altering their securities positions. Interest rates changed quickly, and the anxiety rose. For traders who could read them accurately and go against the trend when others panic, these situations were opportunities for profit. But it is times like these that explain why so few traders have long careers.

Routine Open Market Operations

Regardless of whether the Federal Reserve wishes to fix the level of bank reserves or the Federal funds rate, it must perform numerous routine open market operations that have no policy significance beyond the fact that if they were not done, bank reserves would change by enormous amounts. Commercial bank reserves are subject to several influences besides that of the Desk, and if the Desk is to retain control over reserve availability, it must neutralize these other forces.

A list of the important factors that add or absorb reserves is presented in Table 2-5. Of these, the cash balance of the United States Treasury was until recently the most significant, but since the end of 1978, its role has declined. The Treasury balance can alter bank reserves because cash flows between the public and the Treasury pass through Federal Reserve banks, which act as the Treasury's paying agent. These flows have the effect of open market operations. When the public makes payments to the Treasury, its checks are deposited initially with private banks, in Tax and Loan accounts. The Treasury then calls them into its balance at the Federal Reserve, from which the funds are spent. Between the time of

TABLE 2-5   Factors Supplying and Absorbing Reserves—December 1976

Supplying funds	Amount, $ billions
Federal Reserve portfolio	
U.S. govt. and agency securities	100.3
Acceptances	0.4
Loans to members	0.1
Float	3.5
Gold stock	11.6
Special drawing rights	1.2
All other	15.0
Absorbing reserves	
Currency in circulation	93.7
Treasury cash	0.5
Treasury deposit at Federal Reserve	6.1
Foreign deposits	0.3
Other deposits	1.0
Other Federal Reserve liabilities	3.3
Member bank deposits	26.4

the Treasury call and the expenditures, bank reserves are reduced. The opposite occurs when the Treasury is a net distributor of funds, and its balance with the Federal Reserve runs down. At one time, funds ebbed and flowed from the Treasury deposit in large amounts, often as much as $5 billion or $6 billion in a week. The Open Market Desk had to work against the Treasury flow by temporarily buying securities when the Treasury balance rose and selling them when the balance fell.

The problem for the Desk has been much reduced since the last quarter of 1978, when the Treasury began receiving interest payments on its deposits in private banks, and it adopted the practice of holding its money in them until just before the money is spent. Previous to that time, the Treasury had kept deposits in commercial banks for only a short time because the banks were prohibited from paying interest on them, and the Treasury would have been subsidizing the banks by giving them free deposits. But in November of 1978, new regulations allowed interest to be paid on Treasury Tax and Loan accounts at a rate ¼ percent below the Federal funds rate. As always, the banks must provide collateral by allowing the Treasury to hold an equal amount of government securities. The implications of the new arrangements for reserve management are clear. The movement of money between the public and the Treasury changes the ownership of deposits but leaves the funds within the banking system. The weekly swings in the Treasury balance at the Federal Reserve have been reduced to about $1 billion.

The other source of large fluctuations in bank reserves is Federal Reserve float, which can add or subtract as much as $2 billion or $3 billion in a single day. *Float*, which is defined as the difference between cash items in process of collection and deferred availability cash items on the consolidated balance sheet of the Federal Reserve, arises because the Federal Reserve has established a schedule for check clearing between banks to which actual clearing does not always conform. When someone deposits a check into, say, the Wells Fargo Bank, Wells Fargo adds the deposit to its liabilities, credits its assets with a cash item in process of collection, and forwards the check to the Federal Reserve Bank of San Francisco for clearing. The San Francisco Federal Reserve Bank performs a similar accounting. Upon receipt of the check, it credits its assets with a cash item in process of collection and carries the liability as a deferred availability cash item. If the paying bank, Bankers Trust Company to take an extreme case, makes good on the check within two business days, the transaction is completed: the reserve balance of Wells Fargo is credited; that of Bankers Trust is debited for the same amount; and the Federal Reserve Bank of San Francisco drops both the cash item and the deferred availability item from its books. Float is generated if Bankers Trust does not honor the check within two business days. If the movement of the check across country is delayed, by a holiday perhaps or because a storm closes a major airport, the Wells Fargo Bank still receives credit to its reserve account at the end of the second business day, but the account of Bankers Trust is unaffected until it receives the check. So reserves of the banking system as a whole rise temporarily—until the check actually clears. On the Federal Reserve consolidated balance sheet, cash items in process of collection remain constant, but the deferred availability cash item is transformed into a member bank deposit.

Most of the time Federal Reserve float accounts for between $2.5

billion and $4 billion in bank reserves, although it rises in winter and around major holidays. Occasionally it jumps quickly to $8 or $9 billion, if, for example a storm closes O'Hare Airport in Chicago. When this happens, the Open Market Desk must make matched sale agreements to drain the additional reserves, which otherwise would flood the banking system and drive down the Federal funds rate. The Desk is not always solicitous of the market in these situations and may act regardless of where the funds rate happens to be at the time. Late on a quiet Friday in January, the securities markets can find themselves confronted with a round of matches at what they thought was the midpoint of the funds rate trading range. The reaction is predictable. If the reason for the sales is not apparent, and it never is, the markets go into turmoil, security prices drop, and dozens of weekends are ruined.

Compared to the Treasury balance and float, the other operating factors are relatively unimportant. The public's demand for currency withdraws large amounts of bank reserves, but it has a strong seasonal and is the source of no trouble. During 1977 and 1978, bank reserves were jogged regularly by funds flows in the foreign exchange markets, which in previous years had been of minor importance. The problem arose because the dollar was under chronic pressure, and foreign central banks were intervening to support it. When people who own dollars buy other currencies from foreign central banks, the central banks can do essentially one of two things with the dollars they take in. They have no need for checking accounts, so they acquire special issues of nonmarketable Treasury debt that carry an exchange rate guarantee, or they buy ordinary marketable securities. Whichever they choose, their purchase can alter bank reserves in the United States. If they buy securities in the open market, the dollars are recycled into the banking system, and there is no problem. If, however, they buy the same securities directly from the Federal Reserve, banks lose reserves. Should they select the nonmarketable Treasury issues, and the Treasury deposits the proceeds into its account at the Federal Reserve instead of into the Tax and Loan accounts, banks again lose reserves, and the Desk would have to add a supplement in order to maintain a stable funds rate.

As if these matters were not already complicated enough, a special wrinkle was added in late 1978 and early 1979 by the sale of United States Treasury securities denominated in foreign currencies—the so-called Carter bonds. These were issued for the purpose of supplying the Federal Reserve with foreign currencies it could use to buy the dollar and artificially bolster the dollar's rate of exchange. When the Treasury sold, say, the Deutschmark-denominated issue, it obtained a balance at the Bundesbank in Germany. The Treasury then, in effect, sold this balance to the Federal Reserve in return for dollars, which it promptly spent. The net result was as if the Federal Reserve had bought the securities and added $1 billion to bank reserves. The effects of the Deutschmark sale plus the Swiss franc sale in January 1979, plus the unusually large float added enormous amounts of reserves to the banking system. The Open Market Desk chose to handle the inflow by making outright sales of Treasury bills into the market, a device it rarely employs. The sales constituted a lasting reduction in the Federal Reserve's asset portfolio and a long-term drain of bank reserves. The operation was reversed later in the year, when float subsided and the Federal Reserve sold some of its foreign currency balance.

Besides these relatively exotic operations, the Federal Reserve is in the market regularly as the agent for its foreign customers. The central banks of other countries own over $100 billion worth of Treasury bills, bonds, and notes, the management of which involves countless transactions. All but a handful of central banks do their buying and selling exclusively through the Federal Reserve Bank of New York. The Desk calls dealers to announce it is buying, selling, or performing repurchase or matched sale agreements for a foreign customer. The dealers then submit bids or offers on the proposed transaction, and the Desk selects the best until the order is filled. The Desk also can accommodate foreign orders from the Federal Reserve portfolio, in which case the operations alter bank reserves.

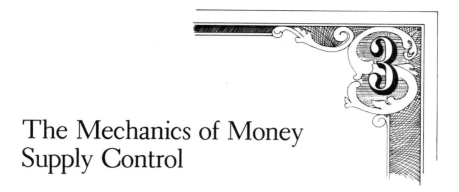

The Mechanics of Money Supply Control

Introduction

Economic changes large enough to require a new monetary policy are relatively rare. During a business cycle lasting three or more years, the Federal Open Market Committee makes at most a half-dozen decisions that could qualify as changes in strategy. And these involve little more than raising or lowering the long-run targets for money supply growth. The Federal Reserve spends the rest of its time designing and implementing means of getting the money supply actually to behave according to plan. It is these tactical measures that consume most of the energy of the Open Market Committee and which have by far the most immediate influence on the securities markets.

The Committee supervises the System's activities from monthly meetings in Washington. For most of the recent past, the fundamental decisions to emerge from these meetings were on the range within which the Federal funds rate would trade during the following weeks and the conditions under which the rate would vary within this prescribed range. Everything else the Committee decided—with regard to open market operations, bank reserves, the discount rate—was contingent upon its choice of a funds rate target. However, late in 1979, a simmering discontent with its inability to control the money supply, piqued by yet another run on the dollar in the exchange markets, moved the Committee to alter its operating methods. It abandoned the Federal funds rate as its principal instrument for guiding the money supply and shifted its emphasis to the growth of member bank reserves. Since then open market operations have endeavored to keep reserves on a predetermined track, and the Federal funds rate has been left to find its own level within a broad range.

These changes set off a period of turmoil from which the securities markets did not quickly recover. The Federal Reserve's switch to a reserves target upset the normal relationships between money, reserves, and interest rates. Securities dealers and professional investors no longer could forecast their own financing costs with their accustomed accuracy, and they required large risk premiums before they would position significant amounts of bonds. After some months, investors learned more about the new system, their confidence returned, and the financial markets regained their previous equilibrium. The rules of the Federal Reserve's new regime ultimately were not difficult to master because money control with a reserves target is much the same as it is with a funds rate target. The new method is little more than the old one modified to permit greater flexibility in the Federal funds rate. After all, the elements of finance are what they are, and beyond certain limits, the Federal Reserve is powerless to alter the ways in which the money supply and interest rates are determined. Then too, reserve targeting and funds rate targeting share a common bond in lagged reserve accounting, which prevents the Open Market Desk from adopting radically new procedures.

This chapter will begin with a description of Federal Reserve procedures as they were practiced before October of 1979, when the Open Market Desk pegged the Federal funds rate. It then will move on to consider the reserve based method of money control. This organization is chosen not to tax the reader's patience with historical detail but because the two systems are fundamentally the same, and an understanding of the currently employed technique will follow naturally from an examination of its predecessor. Besides, a reference to the technicalities of money control with a pegged Federal funds rate might prove valuable for the long run. The Federal Reserve in the past 10 years twice abandoned the funds rate peg, and twice it returned. In 1972, the Committee experimented with a total reserves instrument, and later it moved to a beast called "reserves available against private deposits." Both attempts failed. Its public stake in the present endeavor is much greater than in either of the previous two, and this try might succeed where the others fell short. But then, it might not.

The Open Market Directive

At each meeting the Open Market Committee writes a directive to the Manager for the Domestic Operations at the Federal Reserve Bank of New York, which provides explicit guidelines for open market operations during the period until the next meeting. An example from the period of the controlled funds rate is the one for December 1976. Following a summary of economic conditions it reads:

> At the conclusions of the discussion the committee decided that operations in the period immediately ahead should be directed toward maintaining the money market conditions now prevailing, including a weekly-average Federal funds rate of about 4⅝ percent. With respect to the annual rates of growth in M-1 and M-2 over the December–January period, the Committee specified ranges of 2½ to 6½ percent and 9 to 13 percent, respectively. The members agreed that, if growth in the aggregates should appear to be strong or weak relative to the specified ranges, the weekly-average Federal funds rate might be expected to vary in an orderly fashion within a range of 4¼ to 5 percent. . . .

These wooden sentences held real power. By controlling the Federal funds rate, the Open Market Committee set the terms upon which investors could finance short-term assets. Changes in these costs soon worked forward into market yields and raised or lowered securities prices. In fact, once the message of this particular directive became clear, interest rates rose by as much as 30 basis points within a few days and left dealers and investors with over $100 million in portfolio losses. All that from a document that did little more than instruct the Open Market Desk to manipulate the system's securities in a way that would peg one interest rate, the Federal funds rate, at about 4⅝ percent and to make small adjustments if the money supply promised to grow at faster than a 6½ percent annual rate or slower than a 2½ percent rate over the months of December and January. It also provided for consultation if the funds rate reached the limits of its range and the money supply continued to show strength or weakness. Since the money supply behaved itself, the manager followed orders until the next meeting, when a new directive was issued with a new funds rate target and new money supply tolerances.

These Federal Reserve policy statements were, perhaps, most noteworthy for their simplicity. With all its regulatory and market powers, the Open Market Committee relied almost exclusively upon the Federal funds rate, a rate of which most people are only vaguely aware, as the handle for controlling a $900 billion money supply. One might expect the Committee to employ more elaborate techniques, perhaps involving the discount rate, member bank reserves, or possibly the monetary base. Yet most of these traditional tools were barely mentioned in the directives, and then only as means for achieving the desired funds rate. Implicit in the Federal Reserve's former commitment to the Federal funds rate was a view of how the money supply is determined and of what was the best means of guiding it. In this view, the public's liquidity preference—its desire to hold cash balances—is the central element, and bank reserves, free reserves, the monetary base and all the rest are subordinate to the funds rate. In fact, it can be shown that, when the Open Market Desk fixed the Federal Funds rate, reserve aggregates like the monetary base had no independent influence on the money supply but were instead determined by it. The Federal Reserve reversed the traditional lines of causation.

Liquidity Preference

Most people give the Federal Reserve credit for more power than it actually has—especially with regard to the money supply. The Federal Reserve is not the immediate supplier of money. Commercial banks do that. As a central bank, it controls commercial bank reserves through open market operations, but if the Federal Reserve is to peg the Federal funds rate, it must relinquish this control and give to banks all the reserves they want at the designated rate on Federal funds. Hence, when the Federal Reserve fixes the funds rate nothing stops banks from supplying all the money the public is willing to hold at the prevailing interest rates. And this is the key point: the Federal Reserve's power over money comes not from any mechanical regulation but from its ability to play against the public's liquidity preference by changing these interest rates.

"Liquidity preference" is a general term for the amount of its wealth the public—households, firms, banks, etc.—wants to keep in highly liquid assets. Money is singled out among liquid assets because it is immediately acceptable in payment of debts and because over many years it has demonstrated a close relationship with national income. The actual cash balance of a household or business on any day is the largely accidental outcome of the day's income and receipts, but if the accidents are ironed out and one considers average cash holdings over periods of a month or more, some systematic patterns emerge. A study of liquidity preference is, then, a study of these systematic tendencies in the public's cash balances. The Federal Reserve is aware of these systematic elements and exploits them to control money. It relies upon economic incentive rather than regulatory coersion.

No one really wants to hold money as a financial asset. It pays no interest and, if held as currency, it can be a nuisance to protect. Yet one does not get rid of money easily. Every household, for example, could earn additional income by keeping all of its excess funds in savings instead of a checking account or currency. Few households do this, however, because the advantage of a few dollars income is overwhelmed by the trouble of going to the bank to withdraw funds for each purchase. For most households the inequality is so great they are unaware of making a decision. The appeal of electronic banking is almost entirely that it eliminates trips to the bank and lets people keep more of their funds in interest-bearing form. For a business, the problem is much the same. Instead of going to the bank, they have to pay the salary of a cash manager. This decision, like that of the household, is essentially economic: the income forgone by holding money must be balanced against the cost of its staying invested.

The evidence that the cash holdings of both individuals and firms respond to changing incentives is indisputable. The speed with which NOW accounts catch on whenever they become available is an obvious example; but there are many others. Figure 3-1 plots total money holdings and money relative to total assets among households of different wealth levels. Not surprisingly, wealthier households hold more money. They spend more and have to keep more on hand, and since money is part of wealth one would expect them to have more of it. But as households become richer the share of assets that they keep in money falls sharply.

Essentially the same observations can be made for businesses. Figure 3-2 plots the average cash balance and the ratio of cash to total assets of manufacturing firms of different sizes. Again, total cash increases in absolute magnitude but declines in relative importance as assets become larger. The reasons for these patterns are the same for business enterprises as they are families. Large firms engage in a heavier volume of purchases and sales each year, and they need more cash to cushion temporary imbalances. At the same time, the cost of managing a cash position is relatively fixed. Once

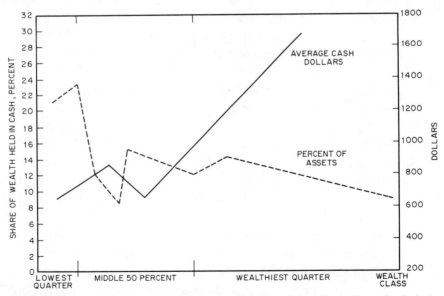

FIGURE 3-1 Wealthy households have more cash but they diversify their investments.

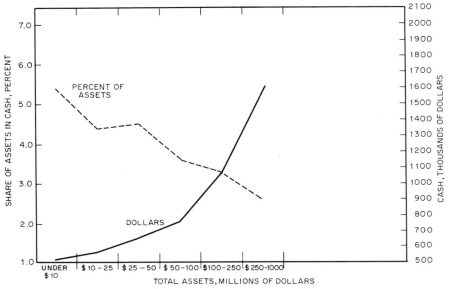

FIGURE 3-2   Large firms hold as little cash as possible.

a company takes on a full-time person to run the liquid asset position, it can have that person manage portfolios of greater size with little additional difficulty. Small firms rarely have a cash manager because the advantages involved are not sufficient to defray a full-time salary. So the smaller companies have proportionately more idle balances lying around than do the larger ones.

The same applies to households. Wealthier ones devote more effort to looking after their investments because the rewards of doing so are larger. Moreover, households with larger portfolios can choose from a wider variety of assets. They have enough invested to achieve a reasonable degree of diversification and so can cope with riskier and higher yielding situations. As a result, they not only earn more income for a given rate of return, but their average return is higher as well.

A similar response to changing incentives can be seen in aggregate data on the nationwide demand for money. Just as individuals and firms who can earn more from their wealth economize on cash, the entire economy tries to reduce its cash holdings as the yields on government securities and other open market assets rise. Figure 3-3 shows this pattern in the ratio of cash to income at different levels

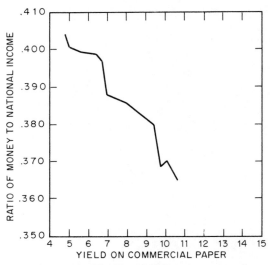

FIGURE 3-3 People hold less money when interest rates are high.

of interest rates. The relationship is not absolutely smooth because other factors, such as uncertainty about future economic conditions, come into play. But overall the picture is clear: the public makes do with less cash as market interest rates go higher, and they allow themselves more cash as market rates fall.

The scale of the vertical axis of Figure 3-3 is reduced purposely to magnify the inverse relationship between interest rates and money. However, the economy-wide response to changes in interest rates is quite small, and understandably so. The evidence on cash economy in Figures 3-1 and 3-2 came from observations across different households and firms, who, because of their size, face permanently different investment opportunities. No matter what the level of market interest rates, wealthier individuals always get higher yields, net of transaction costs, than do less wealthy. However, increases and decreases in the general level of interest rates are never permanent. So, whatever their initial position, most businesses and households try to stay more fully invested as markets rates rise, but they are willing to make only limited adjustments in normal modes of doing business because they know that currently high or low interest rates are not likely to remain. Few businesses that do not already employ a professional cash manager will hire one just to take advantage of cyclically high yields, but they may assign someone to spend a few hours per day overseeing the firm's cash flow. Similarly, people who have never owned a share of stock or a bond are unlikely to be drawn to unusually high yields on Treasury bills, but a few may learn the whereabouts of their Federal Reserve Bank or begin filling noncompetitible tenders at bill auctions. And it is the marginal changes such as these that account for the interest elasticity of cash demands that shows up in the economy-wide data.

Money, Income, and Wealth

If one could identify and weigh all of the factors that influence the public's liquidity preference, interest rates would not lead the list. At best, they would hold the second or third position. Their effects on liquidity preference have been emphasized in the discussion so far because the Federal Reserve relies upon them so heavily. But compared to that of income and wealth, their influence is relatively weak.

The importance of income and wealth is clear and direct. The value of economic exchange rises with national income, and more money is needed to support it. On purely probabilistic grounds, then, as sales and purchases of businesses increase, the chances of their having more funds in demand deposits longer rise as well. This is true even of large corporations, which normally manage their cash carefully, but it is especially true among smaller and medium sized companies.

Beyond the general rise in the number and size of transactions that accompanies a robust economy, the incomes of certain occupations. like salespeople and stock brokers, have especially large cyclical components, rising to great heights during prosperous times but falling sharply during recessions. During the dry spells, the members of these occupations meet many current expenses with funds out of savings, and they delay replacing their automobiles and other household durable goods. During these times when they do little serious shopping and are running down their savings, they maintain only small cash balances. There is little need for a cash reserve when you don't plan to buy anything. But when the cycle turns, their incomes shoot upward, they begin to replace worn-out equipment, and their demand deposits increase in anticipation of purchases soon to be made. This phenomenon occurs to varying degrees in many professions—assembly workers get overtime and the like—but it is most pronounced in the types of occupations mentioned above. At its height, it reinforces the tendency for the money supply to increase during cyclical expansions because of the general rise in transactions. These examples are a few of the channels through which the public's cash balances are pulled up by the economy or drawn down by it. There's nothing subtle about them. They are large and direct, and they account for most of the variation in the public's liquidity needs over the course of a business cycle.

These observations on the influence of income and interest rates on the public's liquidity preference are well documented. The pull of higher income versus the push of interest rates is a conflict that can be found in data going back to the Civil War era in the United States and to even earlier times in countries with longer monetary histories. Given the general predictability of the public's response to changing incentives, the reasons for the Federal Reserve's reliance on the Federal funds rate as means of controlling the money supply are clear. The Open Market Committee has a range of monetary growth rates which it judges to be consistent with the long-term health of the economy. At any given time the Committee recognizes that current economic conditions have a powerful influence on the amount of money people want to have, a force over which the Federal Reserve has no immediate control. In order to offset the influences of income and to make the public's money demand coincide with the money it wants to supply, the Federal Reserve offers the public inducements to economize on cash by varying the level of short-term interest rates. When the economy is expanding and rising incomes pull monetary growth ahead of the Federal Reserve's targets, the authorities raise interest rates and redirect people's liquidity toward other assets. During slumps the Federal Reserve rolls back interest rates and allows the public to relax its vigilance, take on additional cash, and keep the overall money supply growing.

Money Supply Targets and Federal Funds
Rate Targets

This strategy for money supply control is a lot easier to describe than it is to execute. Despite its self-confident image, the Federal Reserve was, and still is, uncertain about the result of its actions. The Open Market Committee never really knows how fast to let the money supply grow in order to keep the economy running smoothly. The state of economic theory is such that the connection between national product, the rate of inflation, and the money supply is not thoroughly understood. And there is a large gray area where the Federal Reserve runs the risk of providing either too much money for price stability or not enough for full employment.

Locating Liquidity Preference

At another level, the relationship between the Federal funds rate and the monetary growth rate often is haphazard. Once it sets its long-run money target, the Federal Reserve has to make an educated guess as to which funds rate would lead to just the right rate of money growth. In fact, the central bank is even uncertain about how rapidly the money supply has grown in the immediate past. Monetary aggregates bob up and down at different seasons of the year, and the problem of distinguishing between seasonal jumps and abiding growth is not trivial.

Still, scholarly reticence does not become a central bank, and large organizations rely upon set procedures and clearly defined objectives. No exception, the Federal Reserve adopted a set of operating procedures involving targets and tolerance ranges for both the money supply and the Federal funds rate which it pursued as if it possessed full knowledge. The hope was that if consistently followed the procedures would on average bring desirable results.

Each meeting of the Open Market Committee began with a staff review of the state of the economy. Recent data on housing starts, personal income, industrial production, price inflation, and the like were analyzed, and the Board staff gave its forecasts for the immediate future, assuming that present policy was maintained. The members of the Committee used this information along with whatever else they might obtain from outside to form an opinion of the general direction of economic activity and of the inflation rate. The review of the economy was intended to answer two questions that are central to monetary policy. First, is the fundamental state of the economy changing in a way that requires a shift toward permanently faster or slower money growth? Evidence may be accumulating that a recession has either begun or will begin soon, or that the economy is entering an inflationary boom. The Committee would meet either prospect by raising or lowering the growth rate of the money supply, not just over the next month or two but for the next year or more. The consequences of such a change would be most strongly felt in the nation's economy, but they also would affect the country's political climate and its relations with other countries. Fortunately, large changes in policy are very infrequent. Between May of 1975, when the Federal Reserve began publishing the record of its policy meetings, and October 1979 there was but one change of great consequence and that was the decision in November 1978 to bring down the growth rate of money and aim for a slower GNP.

The more usual purpose of the economic review was to help locate the economy's liquidity preference schedule. The question here was: if the Federal funds rate remained at its present level how rapidly would the money supply expand during the next quarter or so? The pace of economic activity governs the public's need for cash, and unless the Federal Reserve took countervailing action, an accelerating economy would hasten monetary growth, and a lagging economy would depress it. Even though economic conditions may be essentially satisfactory, the pace of the advance is never uniform. There are periods, sometimes lasting a quarter or more, when activity deviates from its central trend. During such times, the Federal Reserve attempted to prevent the money supply from following the economy off track. It adjusted the level of short-term interest rates to encourage the public to hold cash when the economy dipped and to restrain demand during boomlets. By doing this the Federal Reserve worked against forces that might otherwise have accumulated and caused a temporary deviation from trend to develop into a major turning point.

Besides the strength of recent conditions, the other piece of evidence the Committee had on the public's liquidity needs was the recent history of the money supply. Nothing tells more about the economy's liquidity needs than the money supply itself. In fact, in its policy directive to the Open Market Desk the Committee used recent monetary growth as the principal criterion for deciding when to alter the Federal funds rate. The Committee set tolerance ranges which it believed were generally consistent with its long-run objectives. Monetary aggregates might fluctuate within these ranges without provoking a change in the funds rate. Significant movements outside them implied that the demand for money was either much stronger or weaker than had been presumed, and some adjustment in market interest rates was required.

The setting of these tolerance ranges was an exercise in the true art of policy making. All of the pressures and responsibilities the Committee has to bear materialized in the short-term limits they set for the money supply. It was important that the range not be so wide that money could wander well afield without triggering a correction. Yet an overly narrow range could lead to too frequent changes in the Federal funds rate, build excessive liquidity premiums into market interest rates, and irritate the Federal Reserve's critics in Congress. The problem was complicated further by the fact that circumstances often required short-run tolerances to be established a good distance from the Committee's eventual objectives. So at times extremely slow or rapid monetary growth passed seemingly unnoticed, while at other times small deviations from the long-run path brought a response. The context changed. At times, for example, growth might falter. If the Open Market Committee recognized that the slack was temporary and self correcting, it responded by lowering its short-run tolerances and leaving the Federal funds rate alone. If the disturbance appeared permanent, the tolerances were held and the Federal funds rate adjusted as necessary.

Some appreciation of the decisions involved can be acquired by comparing the policy episodes in the fourth quarter of 1976 with the first quarter of 1978, two periods of subpar economic performance and monetary growth. In 1976, after advancing briskly in the first half of the year, the economy inexplicably sagged. Where real GNP increased at nearly a 9 percent annual rate in the first quarter, it gained only 4 percent in the third. The unemployment rate, which was still a politically sensitive level, stopped falling and was on the rise by September. Somewhat surprisingly, the money supply held up reasonably well. Its growth slowed after June but not to any alarming degree. Nevertheless, by September the Open Market Committee felt it could no longer ignore the economy's weakness. There was no obvious reason for it, nor was there reason to expect it would soon be reversed. At the September meeting, instead of lowering their two-month tolerances and accommodating the monetary slowdown, the Committee kept them near the 6 percent long-run target, and lowered the Federal funds rate by ¼ percentage point during the first week of October, to 5 percent. The money supply had increased by nearly $2 billion during August, but it was flat in September, and the Committee recognized that the public's liquidity preference was waning. They acted to prevent a serious decline in the money supply. The economy continued to deteriorate through most of the fourth quarter, and the Federal funds rate was reduced further, to 4⅝ percent, during December. Conditions then improved, and the funds rate declined no farther.

There is a side point related to this period that illustrates another problem with which the Federal Reserve has to contend: the problem of unreliable data. If one now looks at the reported increases in the economic indicators for October and November 1976, the economy appears to have been robust, and one wonders why the Committee felt the need to reduce the funds rate a second time, in December. However, if one unearths the data that were reported at the time, the picture is very different. Retail sales, for example, appear to have been rising at over a 10 percent annual rate, but as initially reported they were flat. The same is true of industrial production and the money supply during the month of November. If it had then the data as now reported, the Committee probably would not have lowered interest rates after October.

Judging from the existing data, the economy was far weaker during early 1978 than it ever was in 1976. Real GNP was flat for the quarter and, during the first month, retail sales dropped nearly 3 percent and housing starts fell by over 20 percent. The money supply held up well in January, but by mid-March it too had slowed and was little above its level of mid-December. Yet in this situation, which clearly seemed to call for lower interest rates, the central bank did little. In fact, it raised the Federal funds rate, by ¼ percentage point, during the second week of January. Why this seemingly perverse response when the Federal Reserve had eased policy in a less serious situation in 1976?

The two periods were significantly different because in 1978 the Federal Reserve could spot an obvious cause for the economy's weakness: the unusually cold weather that had set into most of the country. So while the economy was in much worse shape than in 1976, the Committee could reasonably expect a reversal. Moreover, in 1978, the economy was into its third year of recovery and, until the weather hit, had shown signs of gaining momentum. A reduction in interest rates most probably would have been only temporary, and by the time the decline had any impact, the economy would be returning to its previous health. The fourth quarter of 1976 held no such promise. The recovery was relatively young and, as capital formation was noticeably slow, it appeared frail. It is important to recognize that, in both cases, the money supply was not the whole determinant of the Committee's actions. They eased in a quarter when the money supply was growing and failed to ease, in fact tightened, when the money supply was stagnant.

Did the Federal Reserve Control Money?

So much for the theory of monetary control. How well did it work? Using the Federal funds rate as its instrument, did the Federal Reserve achieve its monetary objectives? The most powerful theory is of little value if it does not suggest procedures for its own implementation.

Evaluating the Federal Reserve's performance is difficult for two reasons. First is the shortage of data concerning its goals for the money supply. The people who run the Federal Reserve are no less creative than other government officials at finding good reasons to withhold information that can be used to make them look bad. No record of the money supply targets was made public until 1975, when Congress demanded one. As a result, there are but four years of data available, and these cover only the expansion phase of one business cycle—a period of relatively uniform economic conditions. The second problem is that what data there are are ambigiuous. For much of the time since mid-1975, the money supply conformed quite well to the objectives of the Open Market Committee. At other times it exceeded their goals by large amounts. For the four years as a whole, the money supply grew within its prescribed range, but there is reason to believe the Committee was not always candid and sometimes shaded its targets toward the direction in which money was going. So the Federal Reserve's ability to manipulate money was even weaker than the record suggests.

From 1975 until the beginning of 1979, the Federal Reserve defined its targets in terms of four-quarter moving averages. During the first quarter of any year it set the growth rates for M-1 and M-2 that it expected to achieve over the span ending with the fourth quarter of that year. In the second quarter, it set another goal for the period ending with the first quarter of the following year, and so on. Because each target period includes three quarters which also are parts of adjoining periods, if the Federal Reserve brought the money supply in on target over one four-quarter stretch, the odds were good that it would be close in the others. The converse is true as well when it was unsuccessful. In 1979, responding to requirements of the Humphrey-Hawkins Act, the Open Market Committee abandoned the rolling average format and switched to a new procedure that anchors the target period in the fourth quarter of each year.

Table 3-1 below lists the announced targets for M-1 and M-2 for 13 completed periods since the second quarter of 1975. It also shows the actual money growth rates. This record does not exactly flatter the Federal Reserve, but it doesn't damn them either. M-1 has come in as planned during six of the 13 periods. It burst out the top of its boundaries during one disastrous period ending in the third quarter of 1977, remained there through the end of 1978, and then fell back. The recovery from the recession of 1973–1974 began during the second quarter of 1975. The Federal Reserve seems to have kept a firm hold on M-1 during the early stages of the advance, but

TABLE 3-1   Annual Growth Ranges for
Monetary Aggregates

Seasonally Adjusted Annual Percentage Notes

Period	M-1	Actual	M-2	Actual
1975-II to 1976-II	5–7½	5.4	8½–10½	9.6
1975-III to 1976-III	5–7½	4.6	7½–10½	9.3
1975-IV to 1976-IV	4½–7½	5.8	7½–10½	10.9
1976-I to 1977-I	4½–7	6.4	7½–10	11.0
1976-II to 1977-II	4½–7	6.8	7½–9	10.8
1976-III to 1977-III	4½–6½	7.9	7½–10	11.1
1976-IV to 1977-IV	4½–6½	7.9	7–10	9.8
1977-I to 1978-I	4½–6½	7.7	7–9½	8.8
1977-II to 1978-II	4–6½	8.1	7–9½	8.4
1977-III to 1978-III	4–6½	8.7	6½–9	8.8
1977-IV to 1978-IV	4–6½	8.3	6½–9	8.9
1978-I to 1979-I	4–6½	5.5	6½–9	7.2
1978-II to 1979-II	4–6½	4.6	6½–9	7.0

its grip slipped as the economy gained speed. The cash demands of a growing economy exceeded the central bank's expectations, and the Open Market Committee did not raise interest rates quickly enough to bring the money stock into line until the second half of 1978.

The record for M-2 has been better. Earlier in the expansion, while market interest rates were close to those offered on savings deposits, households channeled part of their rising incomes toward savings deposits, and M-2 rose quickly. As the pace of business increased and market rates moved higher, funds were drawn from savings deposits, and M-2 growth moderated. By the middle of 1979, the Federal Reserve had brought M-2 in on target for seven consecutive rolling periods and for nine of the 13. However, even this achievement looks better than it is. While M-2 remained mostly within the official target ranges, it hovered near the upper limits of these ranges, which were themselves too high to check inflation.

Despite a record of modest success, the Federal Reserve bears a reputation of being unable to control money. This opinion is most widespread among monetarist economists, who reason that if the central bank had money under control, inflation wouldn't be as bad

TABLE 3-2 Quarterly Growth
Rates of M-1 and M-2 1975–1979

		M-1	M-2
1975:	I	2.05	6.60
	II	5.25	9.85
	III	7.50	10.40
	IV	3.00	6.95
1976:	I	4.70	10.95
	II	6.50	10.30
	III	4.25	9.10
	IV	7.65	13.20
1977:	I	7.60	11.40
	II	7.70	9.30
	III	9.00	10.40
	IV	7.50	8.10
1978:	I	6.85	7.20
	II	9.50	8.65
	III	8.10	10.10
	IV	4.25	7.85
1979:	I	−2.10	1.75
	II	7.90	8.90

as it is. They also point to the large quarter-to-quarter jumps in the aggregates. Table 3-2 lists the quarterly growth rates of M-1 since mid-1975. Judging from the midpoints of the four-quarter target ranges, the Federal Reserve has aimed for M-1 growth of between 5½ and 6 percent most of the time. Realized growth, however, has been as slow as a −1 percent annual rate and as fast as 10 percent. Even during times when the longer-run objectives have been met, money's side trips off course have been numerous and are a constant source of concern to the Federal Reserve.

This problem of instability in monetary growth is not new. It has plagued monetary policy since aggregates targeting was initiated. Table 3-3 presents the quarterly growth rates of M-1 for 1971 through 1974. The average over that entire period was 6 percent— a rate toward which the monetary authorities probably would point with pride. However, they would be reluctant to take credit for the extreme fluctuations of M-1 around its trend. During these four years money supply growth ranged between a high of 9.3 percent

TABLE 3-3   Quarterly Growth
Rates of M-1 and M-2 1971–1974

		M-1	M-2
1971:	I	7.90	14.70
	II	8.40	14.70
	III	6.95	8.35
	IV	2.80	7.85
1972:	I	8.20	12.60
	II	7.30	10.10
	III	8.75	11.20
	IV	9.35	10.75
1973:	I	8.70	10.10
	II	5.25	7.95
	III	5.85	7.90
	IV	5.45	9.30
1974:	I	7.55	10.75
	II	4.20	7.15
	III	4.00	6.25
	IV	4.65	6.75

and a low of 2.8 percent. Moreover, the same tendency for money to remain above or below trend that was noted in the relatively recent data also appears in the data previous to 1975. Overall, though, while the Federal Reserve's exact targets for the earlier period are not known, they probably were no more successful at hitting them then than they are now.

The Federal Reserve's reluctance to change interest rates has not been the only reason for the erratic behavior of M-1 and M-2. Controlling money has been complicated in recent years by the proliferation of security repurchase agreements, negotiable CDs, money market mutual funds, and several other near-monies that the public can use instead of M-1. The properties of these other assets and the reasons they emerged are discussed in Chapter 4. It is sufficient to say here that all of these other assets pay interest and they are only slightly less liquid than M-1 or M-2. Households and businesses shift their liquidity between M-1 and near-monies as the need arises. When they do, their actions cause large and seemingly arbitrary changes in the growth rates of the official aggregates.

The Federal Reserve has confronted the possibility that the

effective money supply may be something other than M-1 or M-2. Indeed, early in 1980, the Federal Reserve redefined the monetary aggregates to take account of the myriad of financial innovations that has occurred in recent years. While we are well aware of the new definitions, the discussion and analysis in this book focus nevertheless on "old" M-1 and M-2. Over the 1970–1979 period, these were the aggregates of greatest concern to the system. Policy targets were formulated in terms of M-1 and M-2, and the Federal funds rate was manipulated in order to achieve these targets. The empirical evidence relating money to the economy is virtually all framed in terms of M-1 and M-2 as well.

Bank Reserves, the Monetary Base, and the Money Supply

To sum up the preceding section, the Federal Reserve's record on controlling the money supply has been less than awe-inspiring. It has done reasonably well at annual averages, but there have been significant periods when the money supply wandered well off course. The Federal Reserve is aware of its indifferent results and has been continuously in search of better methods. But money supply control is a complicated matter, and good new ideas, on any subject, don't come along every day. However, in the fall of 1979, the Federal Reserve abandoned the Federal funds rate and decided to use bank reserves as the instrument for monetary control. This was not a new idea. It had been assessed by the Federal Reserve many times in the past, and each time it was rejected. However, late 1979 was a time of extraordinary stress. The money supply seemed to be running wild, world bullion and currency markets were burning up with speculation, and the Federal Reserve was losing face by the day. The Open Market Committee needed some bold act that would rebuild its creditability and get the money supply back under control without placing the onus for a 16 or 17 percent funds rate directly upon the Federal Reserve. A move to reserve targeting seemed to meet this need.

If reserve targeting succeeds upon this occasion, it will do so because to control reserves the Federal Reserve will have to let

interest rates fluctuate freely. So, when the public's liquidity preference rises, interest rates will increase more quickly, to prevent the
money supply from growing, and they will fall quickly when liquidity preference fades. Hence, even though reserve targeting holds no
magic, in practice it might overcome the greatest flaw of Federal
funds rate control.

The logic of reserve targeting has an appealing, if superficial, simplicity. Given the reserves that banks must hold against their deposits, there is a mathematical relationship between the amount of
reserves in the banking system and the total amount of deposits the
banking system can accept. To take a simple example, if the
required reserve ratio against demand deposit is 10 percent and the
banks have $100 in reserves, the banking system can accept up to
$1000 in demand deposits. If the Federal Reserve sets the amount
of reserves, it can at least determine the maximum level of demand
deposits. Since the commercial banks rarely hold more than trivial
amounts of reserves beyond their legal requirements, the actual
level of deposits is always near its maximum. So the Federal
Reserve can regulate the amount of deposits by adding or subtracting reserves.

The basis statement of the reserves-based method of money control is

$$D = Rd$$

The level of demand deposits is equal to the product of the quantity
of reserves R and the deposit multiplier d. In the example given
above, the deposit multiplier was 10 because banks had to hold a
dime of reserves for each dollar of deposits. Any change in the
amount of demand deposits outstanding can be attributed to either
a change in bank reserves or a change in the deposit multiplier. Proponents of this approach to money control argue that the Federal
Reserve can control reserves through open market operations.
Then, if the multiplier is either reasonably constant or predictable,
the Federal Reserve can achieve whatever deposit level it wants by
making appropriate adjustments to the supply of reserves. The key
phrases here are *if* the multiplier is constant or predictable and *if*
the Federal Reserve can control reserves.

Without going too deeply into theory, one can find several reasons to doubt the stability of the demand deposit multiplier. As defined above the multiplier is deceptively simple. In fact, it is a complicated expression involving several variable terms. A change in any one of these terms will shift the multiplier, alter the ratio deposits to reserves, and weaken the Federal Reserve's control of money. Of course, the Federal Reserve itself can change the multiplier by raising or lowering the required reserve ratios. These changes are the source of no trouble; it's the changes for which the Federal Reserve is not responsible that cause difficulty. For example, large banks have higher required reserve ratios than small banks. Whenever the flow of business carries deposits among banks in different reserve categories, the average required reserve ratio for the banking system changes, and so does the deposit multiplier. The same thing occurs if people decide to hold more time deposits. Reserves are absorbed by requirements against these deposits and the amount of demand deposits the banking system can accommodate with the same total reserve falls. One could cite several other examples, but the point is that the deposit multiplier is determined by a complex process involving several kinds of financial behavior. It would be only by accident that the multiplier remained constant. However, some of its changes might be predictable, in which event the Federal Reserve could forecast movements in the multiplier and adjust bank reserves to nullify their effect upon the money supply.

Another version of this general strategy employs the monetary base, which is the sum of bank reserves and currency held by the public. Currency is included in the base because it potentially can enter bank reserves if people decide to trade it in for deposits. The ratio of the money supply to the monetary base is called the money multiplier. It is conceptually identical to the deposit multiplier but it is more complicated and less predictable. Whenever the public requires more currency relative to demand deposits, as during the Christmas season, banks lose reserves. Since a dollar of monetary base held as currency adds only one dollar to the money supply but a dollar of reserves is responsible for several dollars of demand deposits, the ratio of the money supply to the monetary base varies as the public holds more or less currency.

Although neither the deposit multiplier nor the money multiplier is constant, some fraction of their movements might be predictable. For example, some of the financial flows that affect the multipliers have strong seasonal patterns and can be anticipated. For a certain group of monetarists, the search for a method to forecast the multiplier has the status of a holy quest, reminiscent of the search for the one true cross. They have devoted thousands of personnel hours and hundreds of hours of computer time to the effort. For years they worked in vain, but recently good progress has been made by applying newly developed statistical methods. The Federal Reserve's success at controlling money depends a good deal upon the accuracy of these forecasts.

Managing Bank Reserves

The format of the Federal Open Market Committee meetings is much the same now as when the Federal Reserve pegged the funds rate. The Committee still reviews recent economic and financial developments and reassesses its long-run money supply targets. However, the Committee's instructions to the Manager for Domestic Operations no longer contain a tight trading range for the Federal funds rate and short-run tolerances for money supply growth. Instead, the instructions stipulate the Committee's targets for money and credit growth over the ensuing months and order the manager to permit bank reserves to increase at a rate that is consistent with these objectives. The directive also contains an initial level of borrowed reserves that are expected to accompany the desired increases in total reserves and a broad trading range for the Federal funds rate. The Federal funds rate would impinge upon efforts to manage reserves only if it hit one of these strike points, which usually are four or five percentage points apart.

The explicit targets for total reserves at which the manager will shoot are developed by staff economists at the Open Market Desk and the Board of Governors. If, for example, the Committee stipulates growth rates for M-1, M-2 and bank credit of 5 percent and 10 percent, respectively, the staff economists make projections for the demand deposits, time and savings deposits, and other reservable liabilities of member banks that are consistent with these aggregate targets. By applying the appropriate required reserve ratios to each liability category and adding a small amount for excess reserves the staff generates a series of weekly figures for total reserves that are implied by the Committee goals for the money supply. By subtracting the initial level of borrowed reserves from the total, they also generate a path for nonborrowed reserves.

Borrowed reserves—loans made by Federal Reserve Banks to members through the discount window—enter the picture as a proxy for the Federal funds rate. Their presence is made necessary by the Federal Reserve regulation that permits members to compute their required reserves each week as percentages of their deposits of two weeks prior. Because of lagged reserve accounting, the required reserves of member banks are preset at the beginning of each statement week. If required reserves should exceed the Desk's target for total reserves, the Desk cannot immediately pull them down. By one means or another, the Federal Reserve must provide its members with enough reserves to meet legal requirements. The most it can do is make banks pay a high price for their reserves, by raising the Federal funds rate, on the supposition that the high price subsequently will curb bank demands.

When the growth of money and credit and, therefore, bank reserves consistently exceeds the Committee's goals, the Open Market Desk continues to provide only those amounts of nonborrowed reserves that are consistent with its initial target path. It thus forces member banks to meet all their additional reserve needs through borrowing at the discount window. Since most banks are careful to conserve their discounting privilege, they will bid actively in the open market before turning to the window. These efforts cause the Federal funds to rise. So the more the Desk forces member banks to borrow, the farther above the discount rate does the funds rate rise.

To the extent they are successful, reserve adjustments alter the money supply by increasing or decreasing the deposits banks can accept. But what happens when the public wants to hold more or less deposits than banks can provide? If they want more, banks consistently need more reserves than the Desk wants to supply by open market operations. Attempting to get reserves but avoid the discount window, they bid up the Federal funds rate and the rate on security repurchase agreements. These higher rates eventually work into Treasury and money market yields and raise them as well. All interest rates rise and play against the public's liquidity preference until people are satisfied with the deposits that banks can supply. The reverse takes place when the Desk supplies more reserves than banks need. If the Federal Reserve is to be strict in its control of reserves and the money supply, it must ignore these yield changes, because to prevent them would require the Desk to add or withdraw reserves from the monetary system and thus surrender its control. The Federal Reserve cannot govern both interest rates and banks reserves.

In short, the Federal Reserve's new method for controlling the money supply relies upon the public's liquidity preference no less than did the former system. The principal, if not the only, difference is that the Open Market Committee no longer accepts direct responsibility for setting the Federal funds rate. In fact, it sets the rate no less than it ever did, but the process now is couched in terms of pursuit of a reserve target with market forces determining the price of reserves. The money supply will behave differently under this new method than it would have under the old only to the extent that interest rates fluctuate more rapidly than they would have had the Federal Reserve retained explicit control of the Federal funds rate.

There is reason to doubt the longevity of the new system. For all the rhetoric about running a policy based on the money supply, some members of the Committee cannot escape the idea that they should control interest rates as well. This position is grossly inconsistent and the arguments against it are legion. Perhaps the best reason for basing countercyclical policy on the money supply is the difficulty in finding the right interest rate for noninflationary growth. Moreover, whatever that rate is, it must be measured after adjustment for expected price inflation, and real interest rates can be neither directly observed nor inferred from market rates alone.

So the Federal Reserve can only guess at whether market rates that prevail at any moment imply a restrictive policy or a stimulative one. These points aside, whether because of political pressure or internal compromise or lack of training, the Committee has never surrendered its fixation with interest rates. When the Federal Reserve restrains rates, it must let the money supply run ahead of target. This is true regardless of whether the control instrument is the bank reserves or the Federal funds rate.

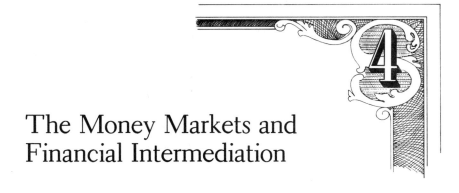

The Money Markets and Financial Intermediation

Introduction

An investor in the United States with a million dollars to place for six months can choose from a dozen different financial instruments and not have to consider anything rated lower than triple-A. The same investor 15 years ago might have had half that range of choice. The difference is due entirely to the new forms of liabilities that have been issued by commercial banks and other financial intermediaries. During the 1960s financial intermediaries somehow recognized the rewards to gaining a more direct control over their own borrowing. Until then most of them had been relatively passive, posting their deposit or paper rates and accomodating their lending to the funds that came their way. Now they pursue every investment that promises the going rate of return, and they find means of raising the necessary money. One requirement of this approach is a variety in their fund-raising instruments that will attract investors with diverse objectives.

Financial institutions also have had to face the problems of a high and fluctuating inflation rate. From the business cycle trough of 1954 to the succeeding peak in 1957, the commercial paper rate increased from just under 1½ percent to something over 4¼ percent. Between analogous dates in 1972 and 1974, the paper rate rose from 4 percent to 12 percent. The difference between the two periods was an inflation rate that was three times as fast in 1974 as in 1957.

The business of financial intermediation could not possibly have been conducted by the same methods during both episodes. Because of inflation intermediaries have had to redesign their loans and find new ways of borrowing. Some of these new liabilities, like negotiable certificates of deposit, serve the purpose of both liability management and inflation finance. Others, like the floating rate note, probably would not be used but for inflation.

The money markets do not exist only to serve the interests of financial institutions. Investors too have been taxed as inflation has driven up interest rates and with them the cost of holding demand deposits and currency. Undoubtedly, they were as receptive to new assets that could serve as money as financial institutions were anxious for new means of raising funds. The synthesis of these objectives is financial innovation.

The Business of Financial Intermediaries

Financial intermediation is at heart a grand play upon the term structure of interest rates and upon the natural aversion of lenders to risk. Ever since commercial banking was invented in 13th century Italy, intermediaries have profited by borrowing short and lending a little longer and by seeking out borrowers to whom their own creditors would not willingly lend. Over the years financial intermediation has evolved into an elaborate assortment of specialized businesses, but each of them stripped to its elements relies upon either or both of the term premium and the risk premium in market yields.

Thrift institutions are perhaps the best illustration of a pure term structure play. In the absence of Federal deposit insurance many thrift institutions would have but little higher credit standing than their individual borrowers. Yet until 1969 they earned a considerable profit from an amazingly simple business. Ninety percent of their liabilities were passbook savings accounts, and an equal fraction of their assets were residential mortgages. Their earnings came from the spread between the interest rates on 20-year investments and demand loans. Since 1969 the thrift business has become a good deal more complicated because inflation has eliminated much of the spread between long- and short-term interest rates. The business also has become a good deal less profitable.

Commercial banks also exist on the spread between short- and long-term interest rates, but they rely less upon the term structure than do thrift institutions and more upon the rewards to bearing risk. Until the late 1960s they too raised 90 percent of their funds through demand deposits and passbook savings accounts, but they diversified their assets much more than the thrift institutions, and their average loan matured in about 18 months instead of 20 years. The rise in inflation has transformed banking almost as much as it has the thrift business, and banks now acquire nearly 30 percent of their funds through the sales of certificates of deposit and long-term bonds, whereas in 1970 these sources provided less than five percent. Of course, these figures are averages for all commercial banks. The money center banks are responsible for nearly all of the innovation in bank finance and rely upon nondeposit sources of funds more heavily than do the smaller banks, many of which are little more than thrift institutions in disguise.

Dealers in government securities probably accept greater risks than any financial intermediary except loan sharks, yet their own credit standing is below that of the assets they hold. Their exposure is to the effects of interest rate changes. They borrow for the shortest possible periods, through overnight security repurchase agreements and call loans from banks. Their assets are bills, bonds, and notes of the U.S. Treasury and of sponsored agencies, which usually yield above the overnight rate and which the dealers buy in the hope of reselling at higher prices.

The Rewards to Bearing Risk and the Cost of Living with It

Market interest rates contain an element of compensation to the lender for the probable loss from default. This risk premium that the lender receives increases with the liklihood that the borrower will be unable to repay the loan. Since commercial banks, thrift institutions, and most other financial intermediaries are more likely to repay their debts than are the parties to whom they lend, there is a natural spread between their borrowing and lending rates that is largely independent of any differences in term to maturity. This spread is their fee for the service of bearing risk. They earn it by employing specially trained personnel and by organizing themselves in such a way that enables them to evaluate certain business risks better than other lenders can.

Large international banks do their best to convey the impression that most of their customers are also large, prestigious businesses. But in reality commercial banks as well as other financial institutions cater to a far humbler cliental. If one were to consolidate the balance sheets of all savings and loan associations, commercial and mutual savings banks, securities dealers, investment banks, and other intermediaries, one would find that their single largest group of customers consists of individuals and families. Savings and loan associations, credit unions, and mutual savings banks deal almost exclusively with families and, at the end of 1978, had $485 billion in loans outstanding to them. Even commercial banks had more loans out to individuals and households than to any other group of borrowers, and the same is true of finance companies. Moreover, the households with whom they deal are not the wealthy. Persons of means have little need for credit or can obtain it elsewhere at rates well below the consumer loan rate. Financial intermediaries concentrate on the middle 60 percent of the income spectrum— persons who are not obviously indigent but who have neither the resources to buy their capital outright nor a personal credit standing of their own.

Essentially the same thing can be said of businesses that borrow from banks, finance companies, and insurance companies. They usually are firms with a credit rating of B or lower. Corporate giants too have large credit lines from commercial banks, but most of those lines are backups for their sales of commercial paper, or the loans they take out of them are made at very competitive rates, leaving small margins for the lenders. The profitable loans are made to firms that can float bonds or commercial paper only in the best of times—if then—or to firms that are too small for bond analysts to bother with. The same holds true in lending to national governments. England and Germany can borrow in the open markets at rates below those which large banks themselves have to pay. Peru and Zaire borrow from the banks.

No doubt some individuals are better risks than many firms, and some small companies are better credits than large ones. In theory, nothing stops them from selling their own paper in the open market and avoiding bank loans, and perhaps certain persons actually could do it—an Aristole Onassis 8½ percent debenture of 1990 perhaps? But the rest would be unable to find a market because size, as much as credit standing, is necessary for access to the public debt markets, and even big spenders do not borrow enough to pay the fixed costs of handling their debt. Foundations, pension funds, and other open market lenders do not have staffs to do credit analysis. Their cost of evaluating a credit would exceed the entire proceeds of a small loan. They rely upon public rating services, published information, and the advice of investment counsel, few of whom pay much attention to small businesses.

Financial intermediaries are better equipped to handle the smaller, riskier loans. They have physical facilities and accounting systems to manage large numbers of relatively small transactions. They specialize in evaluating unusual situations, and they are able to modify loan agreements in ways that improve the prospect of successful repayment. Thinly capitalized firms would run a significant risk of default if they had to meet the debt service of a standard bond or commercial paper issue, but their default risk can be appreciably reduced by a small departure from the standard form, like a delayed payback or prearrangement for contingent financing. Such nonstandardized instruments are of little interest to the manager of a bond portfolio because they are illiquid, but they are the main business of commercial banks, specialized finance companies, and other intermediaries.

The ability to evaluate special risks and to tailor loans is an expensive skill to acquire. Certain finance companies get it by restricting themselves to one or a few industries. Commercial banks have large staffs and extensive branch networks, and they have developed several seemingly eccentric methods that other lenders do not need. The banker-customer relationship so widely dismissed as a vestige of the old school tie is also a necessary forum for exchanging information by which the lender monitors its risk exposure. Compared with some sources of funds banks are high-cost lenders. Blue-chip firms with established credit standing have no need for special treatment. They refuse to pay for it and so use banks only infrequently.

The degree to which firms rely upon open market borrowing versus intermediary loans is not constant. It changes with financial conditions. Commercial banks, finance companies, and insurance companies typically gain a larger share of the business lending during the later phases of business expansions and the initial phases of recessions. Much of this incremental demand comes from medium grade firms that swing between the open market and intermediary lenders. Triple-A companies can sell their paper any time, but firms rated Baa encounter increasing amounts of resistence to their demands as the economic future become more uncertain. When markets become a little ragged these firms are shut out. It isn't that they could not borrow, but they would have to pay so high a rate that their dealers advise them to look elsewhere. Elsewhere usually is a bank or a private placement with an insurance company. Of course, these lenders know they are coming and they prepare in advance to meet the new demand.

The Special Problems of Investment Banks and Securities Dealers

Investment banks and securities dealers confront special problems that set them apart from other financial intermediaries. They play against the term structure of interest rates in much the same way as the others but they have to deal with a different class of risks. They derive income from three general sources: the underwriting fee that borrowers pay to their investment banks, the spread between the average yield on the securities they own and their costs of financing—which is either the security repurchase agreement rate or the dealer loan rate, and the price appreciation of their securities inventories. In these respects they are little different from savings and loan associations, finance companies, or other financial agents. They differ from the others because they bear no credit risk. The quality of their assets usually is as good or, in the case of government securities dealers, better than their own. The risks they take are market risks that arise from the difference between the long-run and short-run elasticity of demand for a particular bond, note, or the commercial paper of a particular company.

The debt of each borrower is to some extent unique. General Motors is the only borrower with the exact properties of General Motors Corporation. The quoted rate on triple-A bonds may be 9 percent, but no particular borrower can be sure that rate applies to its bonds. Moreover, quoted market rates usually hold for trades of a few million dollars. They may or may not represent the rates on a new issue of $100 million. Investment bankers and dealers bet on their ability to estimate the average rate at which a particular bond will sell when fed into the market at a deliberate pace. They base their estimates on day-to-day experience and upon information collected by their sales network. If correct they stand to make a good profit, but once they sign an underwriting agreement or their auction bid is accepted, the bonds are theirs. If they were wrong or if the market turns against them, the losses are theirs as well.

Financial Innovation and the Problem of Rising Interest Rates

In principle, financial intermediaries should be indifferent to the general level of interest rates. So long as the yield curve is upward-sloping and the market gives risk bearing its just reward, the foundations of their profits are safe. The thing that financial intermediaries fear most is a condition of rising interest rates. Since the average maturity on their assets is longer than their liabilities, when interest rates rise, their incomes can never increase fast enough to protect their former profit margins. Of course, financial intermediaries are paid explicitly to accept this risk. If interest rates never rose faster than they were expected to rise, the business of borrowing money for short periods and lending it a little longer would indeed be a simple one. Eventually enough people would get into it to eliminate any chance for real profit. This is why in societies with stable interest rates, like 19th century Europe and early 20th century America, banking was considered a mildly stuffy occupation, where a good family could place a dim son to keep him out of harm's way. But inflation changed all that. During the past 25 years it has driven interest rates higher and caused them to fluctuate more than they have at any time since the Civil War.

Market interest rates contain an inflation premium to repay lenders for the erosion of the purchasing power of their principal during the term of the loan. When the public expects faster inflation, they demand a larger premium and thus force interest rates higher. When they forecast slower inflation, all else equal, they bid rates down. In this regard, a constant, steady rate of price inflation causes few people any trouble. Borrowers, lenders, and intermediaries can eventually adjust to almost any inflation rate. Interest rates rise to reflect the expectation of higher commodity prices, but the spreads between short-term and long-term yields, good credits and poor ones, are unaffected. It is the tendency of prices to rise now faster, now slower that causes problems for financial intermediaries, because it places the spreads between their borrowing and lending rates in a state of constant flux.

Inflation can work itself into interest rates in several ways. In a financial system where the central bank is as active as it is in the United States, a very likely channel is through the effects of inflation on Federal Reserve policy or the market's anticipation of that policy. Investors know that sooner or later high inflation will force the rates on Federal funds and repurchase agreements upward, so in bidding on longer-term securities they demand a margin of protection against the possibility of capital losses. The size of the margin and the periods when it will be needed are very uncertain. Inflation may be only temporarily high, or the Federal Reserve may overreact and bring on a recession, or it may not react at all and the secular trend of inflation may rise.

Considerations such as these and the uncertainty that attends them lead to strange twists in the term structure of interest rates. Sometimes yields rise continuously out of 30 years, other times they rise to two years, and decline thereafter, and sometimes the overnight rate is highest of all. Whatever shape the yield curve takes, the tendency of short rates to rise faster than long ones poses a threat to the earnings of intermediary lenders. Moreover, the possibility of arbitrary shifts in the term structure as the public revises its view of the future is a source of uncertainty that intermediaries prefer to avoid.

Liability Management

At some time about 1970 managers of financial institutions realized that inflation was a permanent problem, and they commenced a search for methods of dealing with its consequences. Most of these new techniques fall into either of two categories—those which fix the rates on their liabilities and those which build in a minimum spread between their borrowing and lending rates. The former include such things as long-term savings certificates, which were insignificant in 1968 but which provided 70 percent of thrift institution funds during 1978. The bonds sold by bank holding companies and longer-term certificates of deposit also are means of locking in borrowing costs and avoiding the overnight markets when interest rates are high. Intermediaries, in general, have moved away from deposits and demand liabilities toward term liabilities. The effects of this drift are shown in Figure 4-1, which plots demand liabilities as a fraction of the total liabilities of commercial banks and thrift institutions. Its pace has varied from year to year with market conditions, but its direction is unmistakable. Insurance companies and securities dealers are omitted from the chart because the term structure of rates is not fundamental to the insurance business, and secu-

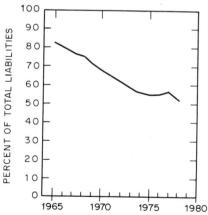

FIGURE 4-1   Banks and thrift institutions cut risk by avoiding short-term debt.

rities dealers have found no ways of altering the term composition of their balance sheets.

To the extent that financial institutions succeed in getting long-term funds, the average terms of the two sides of their balance sheets converge, and they lose some of the earnings from playing against the yield curve. By matching long-term loans against their own longer-term debt, they set a fixed income stream against pre-determined borrowing costs and guard against the losses they would take if short-term interest rates rose more than they predicted. In effect, they choose a steadier but a lower income. Term borrowing also presents the opportunity for a more adventurous financing strategy, which many institutions have accepted. Obviously, the best time to sell long-term CDs is near the bottom of a business cycle when rates are low. The problem is that when long rates are low, short rates are lower still, and borrowers have to carry the proceeds of the CD sales at a loss until their lending rates rise. Banks and finance companies that issue CDs and bonds try to wait for some sign that short-term interest rates have begun their cyclical ascent before going to the market. Thus, for example, they borrowed little in 1975, when short-term rates were falling, but they sought funds in late 1976 and 1977, when it became clearer that they soon could relend at a positive spread.

There is no obvious reason why this strategy should succeed. Since long-term interest rates are averages of the short-term rates the public expects in the future, borrowing long to lend short will be profitable only when bond investors underestimate the levels of future short-term rates. In extending their liabilities, intermediaries pit their judgment against the market's. So far they have been right, because during each of the last three business cycle short-term rates generally have surpassed people's expectations, and the sales of bonds have proven to be a bonanza. There is no necessary reason for this to be true, and over time one would expect it would not be.

Starting in 1974, innovative commercial banks and then finance companies began issuing floating rate notes and CDs which are instruments for sharing the risks of yield curve inversions between borrowers and lenders. The coupon interest rates on floating rate notes are tied, at a fixed spread, to the yield on the three- or six-month Treasury bill. The issuers of these notes are relieved of the burden of carrying a high cost liability if the rates at which they lend should fail to rise. The investors are protected from being stuck with a note whose price would fall far below par if market rates rose more than they expect. Because of this feature, investors will take relatively small spreads—50 basis points is the norm—over the short-term index yield. Commercial banks find floating rate liabilities particularly attractive because their lending rates are based on a three-month market yield, as in the Citibank formula of 150 basis points over the three-month CD rate. Hence, their prime rate is nearly always above the rate they pay on the notes, and at the top of the interest rate cycle, when the three-month rate rises more frequently than the note rate is adjusted, the spread widens to their advantage.

Commercial banks and thrift institutions are further shielded from the effect of yield curve inversions by Regulation Q, which limits the interest rates they pay to depositors. Because of this ceiling, the interest rates depositors receive lag well behind when market rates rise, and banks and thrift institutions have access to large amount of low-cost funds. It also causes them to lose deposits, which must be replaced with market borrowing. Regulation Q, however, has not been quite so large a boon to financial institutions over time as its critics claim. The ceilings themselves have risen over time with the trend of market interest rates, and the rates actually paid a passbook savings accounts, for example, remain near their legislated ceiling even when market rates are below them (see Figure 4-2). Consequently, the average savings rate has approximately matched the 90-day bill rate over the past 10 years. The more insightful criticism of Regulation Q is that it inhibits competition for savings deposits among financial institutions. So while the lobbying organizations of the commercial banks and thrifts have worked hard to prevent the repeal of Regulation Q, they have done so mainly at the behest of their smaller members, who fear the consequences of open rate competition.

The Asset Side

In responding to the vagaries of inflation, intermediaries have found it easier to modify their liabilities than their assets, but those that could do so have adapted their lending behavior as well. Most of

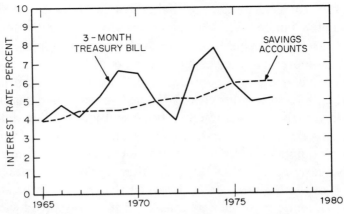

FIGURE 4-2   Deposit rates keep pace with bill yields.

the changes that have taken place, in one way or another, have reduced the average maturity of loans and thereby allowed financial institutions to recontract their lending rates more frequently. The income from loans now remains in closer touch with the current cost of borrowing, and intermediaries avoid some of the cyclical fluctuations in their profits that otherwise would appear. These new forms of lending are additional examples of converging maturities on the asset and liability sides of intermediary balance sheets. They stabilize profits but they also reduce the quantum of service that intermediaries provide, and, as a result, they lower the average yield on capital to their stockholders.

Because they possess the greatest degree of flexibility, commercial banks have gone farthest in redesigning their loans. During the past ten years, they have reduced the fixed rate component of their business loans from more than 80 percent to less than 25 percent. In place of these, banks have substituted either loans of much shorter term or floating rate loans. The interest rate on a floating rate loan is quoted as a spread over the prime rate, which itself often is tied to an open market rate. For example, a loan might be quoted as prime plus one percent, and prime is 150 basis points above the three-week moving average of the rate on 90-day certificates of deposit. Or, in the case of internationally syndicated loans, the lending rate is quoted as a spread over the London interbank rate, which is a Eurodollar equivalent of the Federal funds rate. In either the domestic or international market, the spread over the base rate depends upon the borrower's credit rating. A triple-B firm might have to pay prime plus one percent. A triple-A, because of its access to commercial paper, receives a quote of straight prime or below.

Thrift institutions had for some time done little to shorten the average life of their assets, but since 1978 they have taken several steps. Previous to then, their borrowing rates fluctuated little with market conditions because they were effectively insulated by Regulation Q and by the $10,000 minimum denomination on Treasury bills. Their depositors might want to move funds to higher-yielding assets, but few of them could muster the $10,000. However, by 1978 years of inflation had trivialized the minimum denomination to a point where it was no longer a barrier to large numbers of savers, and thrift institutions were pressed to offer the six-month savings certificate, which has a market-determined yield. From that time onward, savings and loan association and mutual savings banks also became exposed to the risks of fluctuating interest rates.

Within one year of the appearance of new savings certificate, Federal chartered thrift institutions obtained the authority to make floating rate mortgages. The particulars of these loans vary from state to state, but their essential feature is the same as that of a floating rate bank loan, namely, that the lender can modify its terms during the course of the loan. Even this liberty may not protect mortgage lenders during periods of extremely high rates, because the interest rate at which the loan is recontracted is, in most cases, determined by a prearranged spread over the yield on long-term Treasury bonds. If short-term market rates exceed long-term rates, thrifts may yet have to pay more for deposits than they receive in mortgages.

Financial Intermediaries and the Escape from Money

In the United States as well as the other industrialized countries, the issuance of money historically has been a function of commercial banks. It need not be this way, and it is quite possible to imagine financial systems in which money creation is divorced from lending. But so far the provision of demand liabilities which can circulate as legal tender is considered a natural extension of the intermediary role. An important theme in American finance during the past quarter century has been the rising cost of using money and the public's efforts to avoid this expense. Not surprisingly, financial intermediaries have played a major part in these developments.

The public pays for the privilege of holding money in the income they give up by keeping wealth in currency and demand deposits instead of an asset that pays interest. In 1978, the average amount of M-1 in circulation was $354 billion. The yield on three-month Treasury bills, to choose the rate on another very liquid asset, was about 7¼ percent. So people paid nearly $25 billion in forgone interest plus another billion or so in services charges for the unique services of M-1. Using money has not always been so expensive. Before they were stopped by the Banking Act of 1933, commercial banks paid interest on demand deposits, which reduced the income sacrifice involved in keeping ready cash. After they no longer could pay interest directly, commercial banks competed with one another for customer deposits by providing convenient offices, free book-keeping, and other forms of payment in kind. For a long time, the value of these services was reasonable compensation to depositors, but as inflation worked into interest rates, the services became increasingly inadequate (see Figure 4-3). By 1965, the Treasury bill rate was 2½ times its 1950 level, and the public paid $1.4 billion for the use of M-1 that year. The cost continued rising, as interest rates increased until the total expense hit the $25 billion mark in 1978.

One needn't be a great entrepreneur to recognize a business in helping people reduce their expenditures on money. For any product on which people spend $25 billion, there must be some substitute on which they will spend some part of that amount. Understandably, as the cost of using money moved higher, a competition began to develop new financial instruments that would be like money but which would pay interest. The result of this competition has been an assortment of near-monies—negotiable orders of withdrawal, savings accounts that can be transferred automatically into demand deposits, overdraft facilities, overnight security repurchase

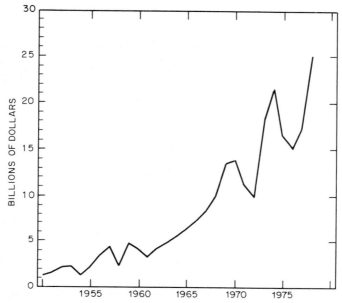

FIGURE 4-3 High interest rates raise the cost of using money.

agreements, one-day commercial paper, remote disbursement systems for moving funds between time and demand deposits, and several others. Each of these instruments provides some of the services of demand deposits or currency—either they can be used as a means of payment or they provide an immediate claim on a demand deposit—and some of them pay interest rates equal to the best available on demand loans.

The creation of near-monies is not confined to commercial banks. Other intermediaries also provide them and actually have an advantage over commercial banks because they are free of reserve requirements. All financial businesses hold some amount of cash reserves for prudence's sake, but they keep less than banks are required to have. In competition they can offer better rates on their liabilities than banks can because they reinvest a larger fraction of the funds they take in, and each dollar is worth more to them. As it happens, however, the most important money substitute for corporations is issued by commercial banks. These are overnight security repurchase agreements and negotiable certificates of deposit.

Banks can pay full competitive rates of interest on repurchase agreements (RPs) because they are not classified as deposit liabilities and no reserves are required against them. More than half of the RPs are for overnight, and banks use them interchangeably with Federal funds. They would be willing to pay a rate up to the Federal funds rate for RPs, but they rarely have to pay that much. Lenders prefer RPs to Federal funds because of the collateral, and as a result the market for RPs is usually 15 to 25 basis points under the funds rate.

Dealers in government and agency securities also issue RPs. They consider RPs the preferred means of financing their inventories because the rate usually is a few basis points below the dealer loan rate from banks. Besides using RPs to finance their own positions, the larger dealers also operate a "matched book." This is a service for customers whereby dealers sell an RP to someone with cash he or she does not want for a day and then do a "reverse RP" with someone who has securities and needs cash. The dealers avoid placing themselves at risk by matching their RPs against their reverses—hence the name matched book. Dealers meet the cost of operating the book by charging slightly more to take in securities than they pay for cash.

No one knows the exact amount of RP securities dealers do every day, but they probably sell at least as much as the commercial banks. Since 1972, securities held under agreement to resell have been the fastest-growing asset on the balance sheets of nonfinancial corporations. In 1978, the corporations held in the neighborhood of $10 billion, and they probably will increase their holdings in the years to come. In 1979, commercial banks introduced a new cash management service that greatly improves the ability of corporations to forecast the volume of checks that will clear their demand deposits each day. With this knowledge, firms can allocate to their demand deposits enough funds to meet these drafts and then place the remainder of their ready cash in RP, where it earns interest. It is difficult to predict how quickly this service will spread to smaller companies, but once it does, corporate cash holdings could decline by more than half of their 1978 level.

Business firms and some individuals did not wait for the development of the repurchase agreement to begin economizing on cash.

They began in the late 1960s to reduce their excess demand deposits and to hold short-term paper instead (see Figure 4-4). The first significant break from cash took place in 1968, when the share of money in the total liquid assets of corporations declined to 56 percent, from its average of about 60 percent during the preceding 10 years. Businesse were lured into commercial paper by the historic high interest rates paper was paying at the time. They subsequently adopted certificates of deposit as their principal money market instrument, but in 1969 they actually sold CDs as fast as they got rid of cash because interest rates on CDs were still constrained by Regulation Q.

Although businesses were drawn into liquid assets initially by their extraordinarily high rate of return, they continued to hold them after rates receded. In fact, they purchased more interest-bearing assets and cut back further on cash, causing the portion of cash in corporate liquid assets to fall even faster in 1971 and 1972 than it had in the two previous years. Corporations found that once they had made the investment of hiring personnel and setting up the overhead to run a liquid asset portfolio they could do it profitably at modest interest rates as well. Then too, the rapid return of high inflation and high interest rates in 1973 probably made them despair of seeing a 2 percent Treasury bill any time soon. Beginning around

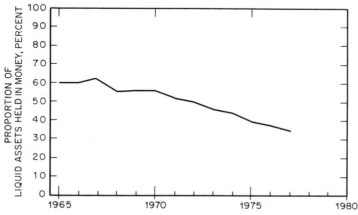

FIGURE 4-4 Corporations get their liquidity in interest-bearing form.

1974 security repurchase agreements took over from CDs as the main money substitute of corporations, although they do a good deal of switching between the two instruments. Their decision on the allocation of funds between CDs and RPs depends upon their interest rate forecast and their need for liquidity. When businesses expect interest rates to remain stable or decline, they move into CDs to ensure themselves the high yields for 30 days or longer. When they expect rates to rise, they move into RP to get a new rate each day as yields rise.

Households too have moved away from money, but with few exceptions they hold savings deposits rather than open market assets. Very few households are in a position to manage marketable securities. The minimum denominations on CDs, commercial paper, and Eurodollars are far out of reach, and until recent years even the $10,000 minimum for Treasury bills was too much for most private investors. Open market investing also involves brokers fees and several other fixed costs and time-consuming procedures that subtract from the net income received by the small investor. Savings deposits have proven to be their best alternative to cash because such deposits have paid a reasonably competitive yield over time, and they can be managed with ease. It comes as no surprise, then, that the rise of savings deposits as a share of household wealth has been the mirror image of the decline of cash (see Figure 4-5).

Only about 15 percent of the households in the United States own appreciable amounts of open market assets. Among them this group controls some 40 percent of the total financial assets held by private investors, so changes in their portfolios lead to perceptible reallocations of the aggregate savings flow. Even these wealthy individuals do not have the incentive to manage their cash as closely as corporations do, but when market rates rise they shift funds away from savings and thrift deposits and into Treasury and agency securities. They also move funds out of common stock and into fixed income investments, but all the evidence indicates that until recent years these large portfolios were responsible for the intermittent flight of funds from depository institutions. Since 1975 they have been joined by individuals of more modest means, who are able in

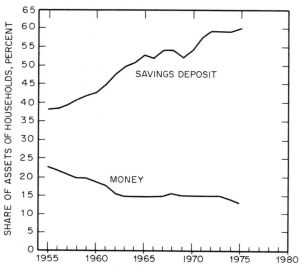

FIGURE 4-5   Money and saving deposits in household portfolios.

increasing numbers to raise $10,000 to take advantage of unusually high interest rates.

Thanks to the persistent efforts of the thrift industry, this disintermediation has joined the Asian flu as something the government thinks it has to prevent, but in fact the financial effects of deposit flight are much overrated. Contrary to the general impression, it does not leave thrift institutions without lendable funds. The Federal Home Loan Banking System exists explicitly to channel funds to thrift institutions when their deposit inflow is insufficient to meet the demand for mortgages. The thrift institutions hate to use the Home Loan Banks, but given the discrepancy between the rates they have to pay for money from the Home Loan Banks and the rates they pay on passbook savings, this is not surprising. In any event, the evils of disintermediation—real or imagined—appeared to have been overcome in 1978 when the Federal Reserve and other regulatory authorities permitted banks and thrift institutions to offer a six-month savings certificate with essentially the same yield as a Treasury bill. This new instrument, while an obvious improvement over passbook savings, has not succeeded quite so completely as it was expected to do because yet another high-yielding competitor has entered the market for household savings. This is the money market mutual fund share, an instrument that offers the saver the same yield as the six-month certificate or better, is available in smaller denominations, and is in many ways more flexible. During 1978 and 1979, the money market funds grew with incredible speed and attracted billions of dollars from thrift institutions, who once again must wrestle with the problem of how to hold deposits.

The Interest Rates on Federal Funds and Other Investments

Introduction

At least once during the term of every President the White House criticizes the Federal Reserve for raising interest rates. Such statements play upon the popular belief that the central bank has power to manipulate interest rates and can set them at will. People who work in the securities markets know otherwise. The Federal Reserve has complete control only over the Federal funds rate, which it uses to regulate the growth of the money stock, but its influence over other market interest rates is at best indirect. Ultimately, the price of credit is set by investors who must set the term upon which they will own the bonds, notes, and paper that other people want to sell. The Federal Reserve can raise or lower interest rates in the overnight markets for Federal funds and repurchase agreements and thereby offer differing incentives for investors to move toward bonds, one-day agreements, or money. It is up to investors to respond to those incentives or to disregard them.

The Rates on Federal Funds and Short-Term Securities

Figure 5-1 documents the extremely close relationship between the Federal funds rate and other money market yields. The numbers plotted there are monthly averages that hide daily changes in yield

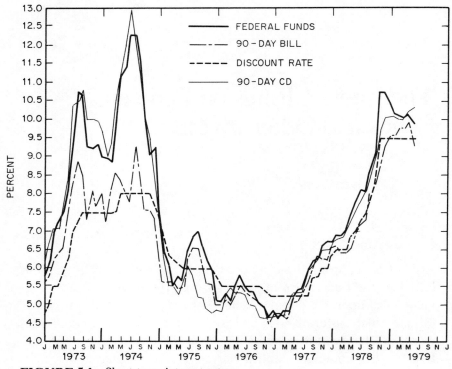

FIGURE 5-1 Short-term interest rates.

spreads, which can be quite large but which cancel each other. People who trade these instruments for their livings often are surprised by how closely these monthly figures move. Accustomed to seeing the markets one day at a time, they are prone to emphasize the special factors in each day's trading rather than the overriding influences that affect all rates in common.

The reason for the near equality among money market interest rates is quite simple—they are all good substitutes for one another in investor portfolios, and money managers switch among them if the move will improve their rates of return. Most of the time the process of asset switching works with remorseless efficiency. Security sellers receive requests from customers for specific issues. They score a coup if they can suggest an equally secure investment with a better yield, or if they can suggest a "swap" in which the customer exchanges a security he or she owns for another that might have a slightly longer term to maturity but a much higher yield. By this process of information exchange obvious good deals are quickly eliminated, and the yields on all securities of the same quality and liquidity are equalized.

Portfolio managers eager for more income move across markets readily. After all, now that inflation has tripled the average level of short-term interest rates, cash management has moved out of the accounting department, and money managers have earnings bogeys just like everyone else. To see how quickly they'll move toward higher yields, one only need observe the changes in the makeup of their investments at different times. Table 5-1 shows the proportional composition of corporate investments at six-month intervals from January 1975 through December 1977. Next to the allotment of each security type is its approximate yield. Note that the yield spreads change very little and do not always agree with realignments of the portfolios. The ease with which funds move among similar assets prevents spreads from becoming larger. As soon as the yield on a particular investment inches upward, money managers buy that security and prevent its yield from going farther.

The base rate in the money market, the one that most professional investors consider their opportunity cost of funds is the Federal funds rate, or, for those investors who do not have access to Federal funds, it is the rate on security repurchase agreements. The two are equivalent except that Federal funds loans are the unsecured liabilities of a commercial bank, while repurchase agreements are collateralized with U.S. government or agency securities and

TABLE 5-1 Composition of Corporate Liquid Assets—1975–1977

	1975		1976		1977	
	Jan.	June	Jan.	June	Jan.	June
Certificates of deposit	53.8 (9.2)	52.4 (5.7)	43.7 (6.0)	40.7 (5.85)	41.9 (4.6)	45.8 (5.5)
Treasury bills	13.9 (7.12)	16.1 (5.45)	24.5 (5.65)	30.4 (5.55)	32.6 (4.4)	23.9 (5.0)
U.S. agency notes	4.0 (7.6)	3.7 (5.0)	2.8 (5.4)	4.5 (5.7)	2.6 (4.5)	5.2 (5.25)
Commercial paper and bankers acceptances	28.3 (9.6)	27.8 (6.0)	28.7 (6.05)	24.4 (6.05)	22.8 (4.8)	25.4 (5.60)

therefore pay ⅛ or ¼ percent less than Federal funds. Both types of loans are negotiable for anywhere from one day to a year, but most transactions are for overnight. Since anyone who can participate in the Federal funds market also can do repurchase agreements, arbitrage between the two markets assures that except for rare instances the yield spread between the two investments just reflects the collateral value of the government securities. Any change in the Federal funds rate is immediately matched by the rate on repurchase agreements, but the latter remains ⅛ to ¼ percent lower.

Whenever the Federal funds and repurchase agreement rates rise or fall the yields on certificates of deposit, Treasury bills and other money market instruments follow suit. But the relationship of these other rates to the overnight markets is very complex, so while the direction of their reaction is easily predictable, the magnitude is not. The most immediate tie between the RP rate and other money market yields goes through the dealer firms that make markets in the securities. The dealers finance their securities inventories by putting them out on RP each day, and they rely upon the positive "carry" between the RP rate and the yields they receive from securities for a good part of their annual profit. Whenever the RP rate rises or falls, the dealers must alter their bid prices to reflect the new cost of financing inventory. Thus, the going prices of outstanding issues are marked up or down and their yields change accordingly. Although the dealers respond immediately, they never know by how much to change their bids or offers. Consequently, after each change in the Federal funds and RP rates a period of experimentation ensues when the markets try several different prices until a new level is found at which portfolio managers and investors are satisfied with their positions and the dealers have inventories of the size they want. The period of adjustment sometimes lasts a few hours, sometimes a few days. After it ends the pace of trading slows down, but even then the markets are never completely static.

Investors continually compare the attractions of CDs, Eurodollars, Treasury bills, and the like against one another and against the advantages of staying in repurchase agreements. The obvious reason to prefer the longer-term investments is their higher yield, but the yield spread required to draw funds out of RPs varies according to several circumstances. When investors move from RPs into any longer-term investment other than a Treasury security, they take on some measure of credit risk. So some part of the yield spread between RPs, and, say, a 90-day CD is a risk premium. Usually it is very small because investors agree that the credit of Morgan Guarantee or General Motors is the near equivalent to the U.S. government's, but the premium increases during periods of financial stress. In 1974, after the party ended at Franklin National Bank, investors were very reluctant to accept the credit of any money center bank. In the overnight market, they demanded a premium of a full 3 percent on Federal funds versus RPs, and they required up to five percent to buy three-month certificates of deposit. This situation was unusual, but not unique. At some time during most business cycles some banks and firms can only sell their paper with a large risk premium.

Besides credit risk, investments of longer than one day also bear a market risk. If the RP rate rises, a 180-day CD bought at a 50 basis point positive carry today can be under water next week. In deciding to move from RPs to longer-dated issues, money managers must assess the probable course of the RP rate during the term of the longer investment. The greater the spreads they demand on long commitments, the more likely is an increase in the RP rate and smaller the more likely is a decline. If the prospects of a fall in RP rate are good enough, spreads between RP and money market rates can become quite small, or if investors sense an important turn, they become negative. Obviously not every investor has the same interest rate forecast. The spread that exists in the market reflects the average forecast of all investors weighted by the capital they control. Considerations of risk aside, those investors who project interest rates to rise less or to fall more than the average are the ones who buy the longer-dated securities. The others either are on the fence or they prefer RPs.

The effects of a change in the Federal funds and RP rates on other money market yields can be analyzed in terms of how they influence the two systematic components of the gaps between RP and the other rates. The credit risk premium comes into play only very seldom. Unless the Federal funds rate rises to extreme heights, it has little impact upon the public's estimate of credit risk. There have been times when tight credit has forced an already tottering business empire down into bankruptcy, as it did Penn Central in 1968 and Franklin National Bank in 1974. But these instances are unusual, and the firms in question were surviving on little more than a shoe shine anyway. But when giants go down, a scare runs through the markets, investors become cautious, and for a few months the yields on all private securities rise relative to Treasury rates.

Except for these unusual episodes short-term yields rise or fall with the Federal funds rate because the change in the funds rate causes investors to adjust their forecasts of the future. The exact manner in which these forecasts will be altered is difficult to predict, and it depends a good deal upon economic conditions at the time the funds rate moves. Perhaps the simplest response would be one in which investors assume that each change in the overnight rate is a unique and isolated event that will not be repeated soon. In this case the spreads between Federal funds, RPs, and other money market yields would be unaffected by the funds rate change, and all short-term rates would rise by the same amount. If three-month CDs were 25 basis points above the RP rate before the change they would be so again after it.

Very few changes in the Federal funds rate are judged to be isolated. Normally, one movement in the funds rate begets expectations of further changes. If, for example, a fall in the rate is accompanied by other news, that economic growth is flagging or that the rate of inflation is on the decline, investors may well anticipate additional reductions in the overnight rates as the Federal Reserve takes additional steps to ease its policies. They would attempt to lock up the higher yields on the 90- or 180-day investments and, in the process, drive those rates downward. After the market had adjusted to the initial change, all interest rates would have fallen, but longer rates would have fallen by more than the overnight rates, reflecting the expectation that the overnight rates would fall again. The variety of investor response to a change in the funds rate is enormous, and attempting to predict it is a frustrating game but an extremely profitable one for those who have the art. As often as not the initial reaction to a new Federal funds rate is perverse. Several times during the cyclical rise of 1977–1979, investors saw the funds rate rise and decided it couldn't go any higher and that the next move would be downward. Yields on Treasury bills, CDs, and other securities rose little if at all. Later, when the Federal funds rate went up again, investors would decide they had seen the interest rate peak too soon; the direction of interest rates was still upward, and they would adjust rates accordingly. The market episode in late summer of 1978 is a very good example of a delayed reaction and then a catch-up. The Federal Reserve brought the funds rate up to 8 percent, from 7¾ percent, after the July meeting of the Open Market Committee, but the market ignored it. Initially, short-term yields moved up a few basis points, but by early August the investing public, encouraged by a public statement from the Chairman of the Board of Governors, became more confident by the day that the cyclical interest rate peak was in view. As the feeling spread a market rally developed, and interest rates across the board fell by between 30 and 60 basis points. At the height of the market even the Treasury's new 30-year bond had fallen to a yield of 8.35 percent, after having traded at an 8.70 percent yield only four weeks earlier. Of course, the fun didn't last. Evidence of the economy's strength poured in. Instead of lowering the Federal funds rate, the central bank raised it in September, and then again in October, and then again in November and then again in December. . . .

The Rates in Overnight Money and Long-Term Bonds

It is safe to say that those who follow the securities markets have known the perplexity that comes from seeing the Federal funds rate rise by a half percent during a week and the yield on long bonds fall 10 basis points. Or during other weeks they have seen the money supply jump by $2 billion, and long bond rates increase 10 basis points. What can be the possible connection between the interest rate on an agreement that lasts 24 hours and another that spans 20 years? No one knows for sure. The best one can do is to note that in a very general way the two move together through time (See

Figure 5-2) and point out a few channels that perhaps can rationalize their loose relationship.

The yield spread between long- and short-term securities is a measure of the slope of the yield curve. Spreads are wide when the curve is upward sloping, narrow when it is flat, and negative when the curve is inverted. Two theories exist that try to explain changes in the slope of the yield curve, but unfortunately neither of them has much empirical power. The two are not mutually exclusive, but adherents to one rarely pay much attention to the other. It's something of a "town versus gown" dispute. Street wisdom prefers the relative supply theory: long-term rates rise relative to short-term when the supply of long-term bonds outstanding increases relative to shorter-term debt. Implicit in this theory is the idea that asset markets are, to some degree, segmented by maturity. There are long-term investors, who only reluctantly buy short securities, and short investors, who rarely extend. When the volume of long-term bonds brought to market exceeds the resources of the "natural"

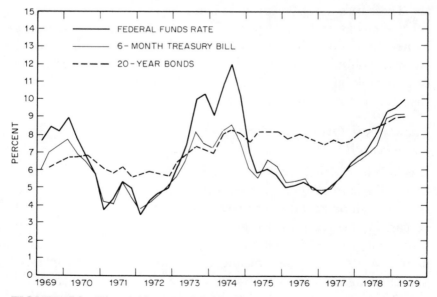

FIGURE 5-2 The yields on Federal funds, six-month bills, and twenty-year bonds.

long-term investors, their yields must rise relative to short rates in order to attract reluctant investors to them.

One source of the supply theory's appeal is its tangibility. One can see amounts of long-term or short-term issues coming to market and feel the strain they place on one end of the yield curve or the other. Unfortunately, while it sounds reasonable the theory seems not to hold much water. It is probably one of the most thoroughly researched topics in the history of finance. The books, articles, and doctoral dissertations written on it, laid end to end, could circle the trading room at Salomon Brothers three times, but however they try, very few can find a systematic relationship between yield spreads and relative supplies of long versus short securities. The evidence just isn't there. Nevertheless, the theory retains its following, often among the very people who undermine it. The belief in sets of natural investors posted along the term spectrum overlooks the role of speculators. When interest rates along one area of the yield curve appear to be too high relative to adjacent securities, speculators sell the nearby issues and buy the higher-yielding ones, thus driving the high rates down and raising the lower ones. Even if investors are somewhat segregated by term, speculators move along the entire curve and, in effect, supplement demand in areas where it is temporarily deficient. And who are these speculators? Wall Street of course.

The alternative explanation of interest rate spreads is not a great deal more satisfying, but at least it isn't obviously incomplete. It postulates that the difference in yield between a one-year and a two-year security, for example, reflects the market's forecast of the one-year rate, one year into the future. The higher people expect the one-year rate will be next year, the larger the spread they demand before buying a two-year security. They would demand it because in committing their capital to the longer-dated issue they are tying it up and surrendering the opportunity to take advantage of the higher one-year rate when it ensues. According to this view, the Federal funds rate affects bond rates by first altering other short-term rates. A consistent series of changes in these rates eventually will shape investor expectations and work forward into longer-term yields.

Besides a general plausibility, the theory has in its favor its ability to accommodate the speculative behavior that is observed among professionals in finance. Speculators have expectations too. Indeed, they have little other work to do but develop them. Unlike legitimate investors, speculators are indifferent to yield to maturity. They are concerned with holding period yield—the sum of coupon receipts plus price appreciation between the day they buy a security and when they sell it, or from when they sell it short until they cover. They scan the yield curve looking for securities with yields that imply higher levels of interest rates in the future than they, the speculators, expect will in fact prevail. These securities they buy and hold for price appreciation. Securities with yields that look low they sell short and buy back later, hopefully at lower prices. Their buying supports the prices and lowers the yield of high-yielding bonds and does the opposite to the low-yielding ones. It may sound from this description as though the expectations of speculators are what set the shape of the yield curve, but that is not so. At times, speculative buying or selling dominates a security market, but eventually speculators who buy a bond must find someone else who is willing to own it. At that point, its yield relative to other securities must be consistent with the expectations of the purchaser. What speculators in fact do is provide a risk-bearing service. They give temporary support to areas of the yield curve that are under pressure, possibly because of a large new supply. It isn't that they perceive value in those bonds to which the rest of the world is blind. The market pays them a fee to bring the yield curve into line with the consensus forecast and while they are doing it to face the consequences if that forecast is wrong.

In practice, the speculator role is played by two groups of market participants. The first includes securities dealers and underwriters who make markets in bonds. Part of their job is to know what yield a bond will have to pay to sell in a given financial environment. When a particular issue meets resistance, possibly because the market is crowded or temporarily disrupted, they hold the bond in inventory until either normal market conditions return or their view of the underlying course of interest rates is proved wrong. The other group consists of trading portfolios. Often they are commercial banks or corporations, like First Union Bank of North Carolina or First National Bank of Chicago or Ford Motor Company. Their primary interest is buying securities to hold until maturity, but they commit some fraction of their resources to buying securities that appear to be underpriced relative to the trend of interest rates. These they hold for a short while and resell when their prices rise.

The utility value of the expectations theory is limited because interest rate expectations cannot be directly measured. They can only be inferred after the fact from the spreads between short-term and longer-term interest rates. Since they represent a state of mind they cannot be observed independently of these spreads, a fact which makes the expectations theory as much a rationalization as an explanation. These qualifications aside, it still provides a convenient framework for analyzing the effects of Federal funds rate changes on the yields of bonds and long-term notes.

It is clear from Figure 5-1 that the Federal funds rate substantially dominates the rates on commercial paper, CDs, Eurodollar CDs, and other short-term paper. The impact of the funds rate on longer-term investment is less direct. It depends upon the effect of any given change in short-term rates on investor expectations of additional changes in the future. These effects fall into three general classes: those changes the market disregards as likely to be reversed, those the market sees as part of the ordinary cycle of interest rates, and those which represent fundamental changes in the direction of monetary policy. Examples of the first type—the false starts—usually occur when the Federal Reserve forecasts one thing for the economy, and the investing public forecasts the opposite. In the spring of 1975 the economy was just recovering from the worst recession in 40 years. Most businesses were reporting mediocre results, and few people felt certain the advance would be sustained. Responding to a quick jump in the money supply, the Federal Reserve raised the Federal funds rate 90 basis points between May and August. The rate on 90-day certificates of deposit rose by an equal amount, and the Treasury bill rate went up by somewhat more. The Treasury bond rate, however, rose seven basis points. In fact, it declined after the initial funds rate move, but it belatedly followed in August. Investors did not see the strength in the economy that the Federal Reserve saw and they refused to agree that interest rates had begun their cyclical ascent. And they were right! In September the Federal funds rate turned around and by November it was back to the level of May.

Between January of 1976 and September 1977, investors chose to ignore three additional increases in short-term interest rates, and in each case they did so for essentially the same reasons—the advance of the real economy was unconvincing, and the rate of price inflation seemed to be declining. In the first of those three incidents, they were correct; the higher short-term rates did not hold up. The other two, in retrospect, were mistakes. In September of 1977, after the real GNP had advanced by more than 5 percent for three consecutive quarters and the rate of inflation was accelerating, the public finally saw things in the Federal Reserve's way. Borrowers began coming into the bond markets before rates moved higher, and investors began avoiding bonds for fear of capital losses. As a result, the yield on 30-year government bonds rose by 150 basis points over the next nine months. A mistaken recession caused then to decline briefly in the late summer of 1978, but they then rose another 100 basis points by May of 1979.

Examples of the third class of reaction—one that anticipates a new direction for monetary policy—are difficult to cite because policy changes are so infrequent. Cynics would argue there have been none for 20 years; the Federal Reserve has been inflationary the entire time. At some point in the early 1960's the Federal Reserve must have decided it could pursue a more expansive policy. By 1964 the wholesale price index actually had been declining for three years, and adjusted for quality changes, consumer prices probably were falling as well. The economy had run with some measure of excess capacity for several years, and the benefits of faster economic growth were much discussed. When the central bank altered its long-run stance the implications for the price level were profound. However, they went unnoticed. Apparently misled by the optimistic rhetoric of the time and words like "fine tuning" that began showing up in memoranda at the Brookings Institution, investors didn't see the inflation consequences, and the term structure of interest rates barely budged. Those few who did see the dangers were branded as Gold Bugs and were tolerated as colorful oddballs in a liberal society.

On a smaller scale, investors gradually have learned that the Federal Reserve is a principal cause of cyclical fluctuations in the economy. They have become increasingly watchful for those changes in Federal Reserve operations that might announce the cycle turning point. Large increases in the Federal funds rate late in business expansions tend to get this interpretation, and they either leave long-term interest rates unchanged or they cause them to fall, as investors foresee higher unemployment and weaker credit demands. Since there can be only one turn in each cycle, odds are that the market will make several false starts before the real turn arrives. Investors who recognize them as such can make a year's profit in a few months time, because interest rates recoil quickly when people realize they have once again been looking in the wrong place and the pea is under the other shell.

Money-Sensitive Sectors
of the Economy

Introduction

For monetary policy to be effective, it must influence the amounts of money that people spend. Undoubtedly, in recent years businesspeople and consumers have come to believe that large changes in the money supply, in one direction or the other, foreshadow changes in business conditions. But expectations by themselves are not enough. Eventually monetary policy must also influence actions—spending and investment decisions—or else participants would ultimately conclude that it really didn't matter. In this chapter we report evidence demonstrating the potency of monetary policy and then we look systematically at major sections of the economy, to see where monetary policy has an influence and how that influence might operate. Logically, this chapter provides the sector detail that underpins some of the results cited at the outset of the book, for if the money supply influences the course of the aggregate economy, it must affect one or more of its major sectors.

Big Noise from St. Louis

Some of the most convincing evidence regarding the influence of money and monetary policy was developed by the Federal Reserve Bank of St. Louis in the late 1960s. One of the really striking features of this analysis is that it has withstood criticism and scrutiny for more than ten years with most of its major conclusions intact.

As we shall see, though, there are still several questions raised by the St. Louis results that have not as yet been answered satisfactorily.

In Table 6-1, we show the impact of monetary policy on the economy, as estimated by Jerry Jordan and Leonall C. Andersen of the St. Louis Federal Reserve Bank. The evidence says that a once and for all increase in the money supply of, say, $1 billion is associated with a $1.6 billion increase in GNP in the contemporaneous quarter and a $6.6 billion advance—which is the full effect—during the next four quarters.

These estimates indicate that monetary policy is much more powerful and acts more quickly than many analysts had previously believed. For example, when this analysis appeared in 1968, the conventional wisdom held that monetary policy had no detectable impact on the economy within a year, and that the total effect after three years was probably only about $2 billion of additional GNP for each $1 billion of additional money.

Not only were the St. Louis results revolutionary with regard to monetary policy, but assumptions about fiscal policy were overturned as well. The St. Louis economists found that fiscal policy, whether measured as Federal spending or tax changes, had virtually no lasting impact on the economy. Increases in the Federal deficit give the economy an initial boost, but they also cause higher interest rates, which later crowd out private spending. Previously, of course, fiscal policy had been considered very potent, and indeed

TABLE 6-1   Impact of Money on GNP

"St. Louis Results"

Elapsed time	Multiplier*
After 1 quarter	1.6
After 2 quarters	3.5
After 4 quarters	6.6
After 12 quarters	6.6

*The money multiplier shows the change in the level of GNP after the time period specified associated with a once and for all increase in the level of the money supply of $1.0 billion.

much recent work by the economics profession has been devoted to resurrecting fiscal policy. The effectiveness of fiscal policy, as estimated by the St. Louis economists, is reported in Table 6-2. A $1 billion increase in government expenditures or a $1 billion reduction in taxes has negligible impact on the economy.

The Federal Reserve is far too cautious an institution to be moved by a single piece of evidence. The St. Louis equations were influential because they came at a strategic moment. Signs of money's power over economic events had been accumulating for many years, and the St. Louis model provided a final dramatic demonstration. Its critics called the model simpleminded. It is, but it withstood their attacks, and the Federal Reserve went over to aggregates policy two years after its publication. While the St. Louis results build the case for monetary policy, they leave unanswered the question of how money affects spending. We look next at specific sectors and their relation to policy changes.

Residential Construction

There is widespread agreement that monetary policy can influence new building of single-family and multifamily dwellings. In fact, it is generally maintained that housing "takes it on the chin" during periods of monetary restraint, and rebounds as strongly when money eases. But there is sharp disagreement as to just how these swings in homebuilding are brought about.

Interestingly enough, there is a good simple explanation for the vulnerability of homebuilding to monetary policy. Yet many econ-

TABLE 6-2   Fiscal Policy Effects on GNP*

"St. Louis Results"

Elapsed time	Federal government spending	Federal government taxes
After 1 quarter	0.4	0.2
After 2 quarters	0.9	0.2
After 4 quarters	0.1	0.2
After 12 quarters	0.1	0.2

*These figures show the effects of a $1.0 billion increase in Federal spending, or $1.0 billion decrease in taxes, on GNP after the time period specified.

omists and most nonprofessionals adhere to a convoluted and improbable explanation that is often called the "availability doctrine."

According to this approach, it is the availability, or lack thereof, of mortgage money which determines the course of homebuilding activity. When mortgages are available, housing starts will be strong, irrespective of prevailing and prospective levels of interest rates. But if mortgage finance is unavailable, then housing will be in the doldrums, presumably because potential homebuyers cannot obtain mortgages.

Since savings and loan associations (S&Ls) and mutual savings banks (MSBs) are major lenders in the mortgage market, they are crucial in making mortgage money available. And it is here that monetary policy can be very powerful, for if the Federal Reserve pushes market interest rates above rates that these institutions can pay their depositors, then they will be unable to attract new money and may lose a portion of their old.

This process, known as disintermediation, occurs when market interest rates exceed rates offered by S&Ls and MSBs, whose competitive position is restricted by government-imposed interest rate ceilings. As new money dries up, according to this theory, mortgage lending is curtailed and housing suffers. Even without interest rate ceilings, the process of disintermediation could occur, for thrift institutions might not be able to compete effectively during high rate periods, since they hold mostly long-term assets and cannot afford a substantial jump in the cost of short-term deposits.

Indeed, thrifts used to benefit regularly from the normal upward-sloping yield curve, which indicated higher returns on long-term relative to short-term assets. However, with the advent of persistently high inflation and frequent bouts of monetary restraint, periods of inverted yield curves have become more common, much to the detriment of thrift institution profitability.

The availability view we have been describing has held sway for a long time, and the government has created a number of agencies to try to help stabilize housing finance. Thus, FNMA, GNMA, and FHLMC were created to provide funds for housing when they otherwise might be difficult to obtain. The magnitude of the operations of these agencies is summarized in Table 6-3.

TABLE 6-3 Major Sources of Mortgage Finance

($ Billions)

Sector	1964	1965	1966	1967	1968	1969	1970	1971	1972	1973	1974	1975	1976	1977	1978	1979
Savings and loan associations	8.1	7.1	2.8	5.8	6.8	7.7	6.8	6.4	24.6	21.5	13.9	23.2	37.3	49.9	45.5	37.2
Mutual savings banks	3.0	3.0	1.8	2.0	1.6	1.6	1.1	1.2	2.7	2.6	0.7	0.8	2.8	4.5	4.6	2.4
Commercial banks	2.3	3.2	2.4	2.5	3.5	2.9	0.9	5.7	9.0	11.0	6.6	2.1	8.8	18.7	21.9	19.1
Mortgage pools*		0.1	0.3	0.5	0.4	0.4	1.2	4.3	4.3	3.2	5.4	9.9	14.5	19.0	15.8	23.5
Sponsored credit agencies†	−0.1	0.5	1.9	1.1	1.6	3.8	4.6	2.1	1.8	3.5	5.5	2.5	0.5	0.5	9.0	9.2
Households	1.6	1.2	1.4	1.6	2.5	2.0	−0.1	3.0	3.3	3.0	2.4	2.5	4.5	9.0	8.4	7.8
Federal government	−0.1	−0.1	0.6	0.7	0.9	0.2	−0.1	−0.6	−0.6	−0.8	0.8	1.9	−2.8	−0.3	−1.0	0.2
Insurance companies	1.7	1.7	1.2	−0.2	−0.6	−1.3	−0.8	−2.3	−2.7	−2.0	−1.4	−1.9	−1.6	−1.4	−0.3	0.9

*GNMA, FHLMC, and FHA guaranteed securities.
†FNMA, FHLMC, and FLB.

As you can see in rows 4 and 5 of Table 6-3, government credit activity in support of mortgages has increased materially in recent years. The sponsored agencies provided $9 billion of funds in 1978 and $9.2 billion in 1979. The growth in the activity of mortgage pools has been even greater, climbing from the $3 to $4 billion range in the early 1970s to $23.5 billion in 1979.

"Ginnie Mae" and "Freddie Mac" sell their own obligation in the open market and provide funds to private institutions, thus replacing the funds thrifts lose by deposit outflow. Such activities, along with the normal lending of the Federal Home Loan Banks, maintain the liquidity of Savings and Loan Associations and Mutual Savings Banks during periods of credit stringency and assure mortgage funds to all borrowers who are willing to pay the price.

Within the private sector, thrift institutions and their investment bankers have developed techniques to improve liquidity and enable them to continue to grant mortgages even during periods of high interest rates—hence the advent of mortgage-backed bonds, of privately insured mortgage pools, and of housing finance agencies at the state and local level.

Problems continue to arise, however. Some states have usury ceilings on mortgage interest rates, and lenders in those states frequently prefer high-yielding GNMA securities to local mortgages that are "capped." Equally significant is the effect known as "marginal disintermediation." This term describes the general tendency for funds to flow to open market instruments, as opposed to financial intermediaries, as new instruments are created and yields in the market rise. Thus, with Ginnie Maes, Freddie Macs, and private packages as well, competition for the saving dollar is enhanced and the aggregate benefits to the mortgage market may not be as large as sometimes claimed.

Indeed, if it is primarily credit availability that matters for housing, then homebuilding should in the future be less vulnerable to monetary restraint. Not only should the instruments and agencies mentioned above succeed in protecting housing if availability is crucial, but the emergence of money market certificates offered by thrifts, as well as other financial innovations, should improve the stability of deposit flows as well.

From the point of view of the S&Ls at least, and they are the major institution in the market, 1966 was the worst year they experienced in terms of deposits (see Table 6-4). Since that time, "credit crunches" have not been as severe, and yet housing has continued to swing violently over the business cycle.

This suggests that there are factors other than availability at work. Indeed, the emphasis on availability may well be misguided and may have obscured more fundamental determinants of home-building activity.

The classical view of the relation between monetary policy and housing points to a key feature of spending on residential construction, namely, that it is a capital item that is postponable when real interest rates are high. Unlike food and other necessities, the desire

TABLE 6-4 Deposit Changes at Savings and Loan Associations

During Periods of "Tight Money"

Period		Increase or decrease in deposits, $ billions	Increase or decrease as % of deposits
1966:	I	+1.3	1.2
	II	+0.7	0.7
	III	−0.7	0.6
	IV	+2.2	2.0
1969:	I	+0.9	0.7
	II	−0.1	0.1
	III	−1.3	1.0
	IV	−0.6	0.5
1970:	I	−0.7	0.5
	II	+1.2	0.9
	III	+1.6	1.2
	IV	+3.3	2.4
1973:	I	+6.5	3.2
	II	+3.4	1.6
	III	−1.8	0.8
	IV	+2.4	1.1
1974:	I	+5.5	2.5
	II	+0.1	a
	III	−2.9	1.3
	IV	+2.0	0.9

[a]Less than 0.1%.

to move to a new, larger house or apartment can be deferred if need be. And the principal reason for such deferral is high interest rates.

In many cases, it is not a move from inadequate to adequate housing that is at stake, but rather a step up to larger quarters, which is readily deferred. The size of the down payment typically stiffens during periods of restraint and a home owner with, say, an 8 percent mortgage on his or her current house may be very reluctant to move and take on new financing at perhaps 10 percent. Of course, the home owner may be able to refinance subsequently at a lower rate, but in inflationary times this is an uncertain prospect. In a sense, then, the home owner behaves as if he or she were "locked in."

Aside from these secondary considerations, the key financial variable in the housing decision is the real interest rate—that is, the margin by which the quoted interest rate on mortgages exceeds the likely price appreciation of houses. The rise of a few percent in the mortgage rate will not restrain housing demand if the increase represents nothing more than faster inflation. But when interest rates rise above the inflation rate, house buyers step out of the market.

This is not to say that interest rates are all that "matter" for housing, or that housing units are permanently lost due to restrictive policies. In the longer run, for example, demographic factors, especially the percentage of the population in the 25- to 44-year-old age bracket, are a major determinant of housing activity. Thus, the postwar baby boom which is now working its way through this age group should provide powerful upward momentum to new homebuilding. Restrictive monetary policy may alter the timing of the satisfaction of this demand, but it seems likely that it will ultimately be met.

To return to the issue at hand, in Tables 6-5 and 6-6 we have depicted measures of housing activity, monetary policy, and overall economic performance. This evidence demonstrates some of the relations we have discussed, and also shows that homebuilding usually moves before the economy as a whole.

For example, if we look at the housing starts and permits rows in Table 6-5, we see that these measures almost always bottom out before the economy, as measured by real GNP. This relationship is even more obvious in Table 6-6, which of course refers to peaks in economic activity and other variables.

TABLE 6-5 Specific Trough Dates Corresponding to Expansions Beginning in Various Months

	March 1975	Nov. 1970	Feb. 1961	April 1958	May 1954
Real GNP	1975-I	1970-IV	1961-I	1958-I	1954-II
Real residential construction	1975-I	1970-II	1960-IV	1958-I	1953-IV
Housing starts	2/75 (−1)	1/70 (−10)	12/60 (−2)	2/58 (−2)	8/53 (−9)
New permits (private housing)	3/75 (0)	1/70 (−10)	12/60 (−2)	2/58 (−2)	9/53 (−8)
3-Month T bill rate	4/77 (+25)	3/71 (+4)	1/61 (−1)	6/58 (+2)	6/54 (+1)
Mortgage yields, secondary market	12/76 (+21)	3/71 (+4)	5/63 (+27)	7/58 (+3)	7/54 (+2)
Real M-2	2/75 (−1)	2/70 (−9)	5/60 (−9)	1/58 (−3)	na

NOTE: Numbers in parentheses indicate leads (−) or lags (+) of specific dates in relation to reference dates.

The jury is still out on the "availability versus classical" debate, but we favor the classical position ourselves. There is no question but that housing is a long-lived capital good whose purchase can be deferred during periods of high interest rates. Moreover, the pop-

TABLE 6-6 Specific Peak Dates Corresponding to Contractions Beginning in Various Months

	Nov. 1973	Dec. 1969	April 1960	Aug. 1957	July 1953
Real GNP	1973-IV	1969-III	1960-I	1957-III	1953-II
Real residential construction	1973-I	1969-I	1959-II	1955-II	1953-II
Housing starts	1/72 (−22)	1/69 (−11)	2/59 (−13)	12/54 (−32)	na
Permits	12/72 (−11)	2/69 (−10)	11/58 (−17)	2/55 (−30)	11/52 (−8)
3-Month T bill rate	8/74 (+9)	1/70 (+1)	12/59 (−4)	10/57 (+2)	4/53 (−3)
Mortgage yields, secondary market	9/74 (+10)	2/70 (+2)	1/60 (−3)	10/57 (+2)	9/53 (+2)
Real M-2	7/73 (−4)	2/69 (−10)	7/59 (−9)	4/56 (−16)	na

NOTE: Numbers in parentheses indicate leads (−) or lags (+) of specific dates in relation to reference dates.

ular linkage between mortgage credit and residential construction spending seems strained, to say the least, since we are aware of no other area of aggregate demand where the availability of credit is thought to be a major determinant.

Consumer Durable Spending

Spending by households on durable goods—autos, furniture, appliances, and like—may be sensitive to monetary policy as well, although the route of influence may be circuitous. Such purchases are of course frequently financed with external funds, so the cost of borrowing enters in. The interest rate on installment credit is insensitive to overall monetary conditions, but not everyone uses installment credit. Many people finance their equipment purchases with personal loans or loans against securities, the rates on which move closely with market yields.

Many consumer durables are complementary with housing. That is, appliance and furniture expenditures frequently go hand-in-hand with a move to a new or larger home, and when residential construction activity is curtailed by monetary restraint, these related expenditures decline as well.

Where money may also play a forceful role is in the so-called wealth effect. That is, consumer durable spending depends upon things other than current income, household wealth among them. To see this, suppose the Rockefellers had no current income—their consumption of durables, or anything else, would scarcely be affected, because they can spend their wealth.

One prominent way in which monetary policy may influence household wealth is through its effects on common stock prices. The stock market crash in October 1929 is considered a major factor in the decline in household wealth and attendant drop in consumption spending during the depression. But what of the relation between money and stocks? Here the battle rages.

There are many theories of stock price determination, none of which seem entirely satisfactory. However, most studies find some positive effect of monetary conditions upon equity prices, and a few claim the influence is quite large. Without going into great detail, bull markets in common stock tend to coincide with periods of expansionary monetary policy, as happened in 1964–66, 1968, 1971–72, and 1975–76. Periods of restrictive policy also accompany bear markets, as was the case in 1967, 1970, and 1973–74. The channels by which money influences stock prices, however, are unclear. Several things occur more or less at once. Rapid money growth raises the public's overall liquidity and encourages speculative investing. Then too, if other parts of the economy also respond to stimulative policy, the prospects for corporate earnings improve, and the makings for a bull market fall into place. The rise in stock prices adds to the public's perceived wealth, encourages spending, and the process gains momentum.

Tight financial conditions have the reverse effect. They lead to lower earnings forecasts and attract investors into high-yielding short-term investments.

At one time investment advisors would tout common stock as a hedge against inflation. Investors who followed that advice found it a formula for financial ruin—not because corporate earnings do not rise with the price level, but because several other factors have accompanied inflation that have swamped the effects of higher earnings. One of these has been greater volatility in the economy's performance that has made investors reluctant to commit their funds to illiquid investments and to discount future incomes by a larger factor. As a result the persistently expansive monetary policy of the past 10 years has led to lower stock prices rather than the higher prices that investment analysts of the 1950's would have predicted.

It would seem, then, that we have to distinguish between short- and long-run influences of money on the stock market. In the short run, the liquidity effect dominates, suggesting a positive relation between money and equity values. But in the longer run, volatile money growth may well depress equities, as investors demand higher returns in an uncertain economic environment. And through these influences, consumer spending may be stimulated or restrained as the stock component of wealth varies.

One intriguing implication that follows from this discussion relates to the analysis of money and the business cycle, cited earlier. Empirical evidence indicates that significant decelerations in growth in the monetary aggregates is accompanied by peaks in business activity. That is, recessions and slowdowns in monetary growth apparently go hand in hand.

We also know that stock prices are a good leading indicator of economic activity, rising or falling before the economy does. Taken together, these relationships suggest that volatility in money growth depresses stock prices, and this effect, in turn, feeds into spending decisions, contributing to weakness in the economy. Furthermore, it is interesting to note that while the stock market usually turns down before the economy, it also tends to perk up before the economy begins to recover. This may reflect the positive effects of reduced money growth on inflation premia in interest rates, but obviously until further evidence is developed we are getting into rather speculative territory.

Money and Interest Rates

Closely related to the foregoing discussion is the nature of the relationship between the money supply and interest rates. In the old days, the analysis rarely proceeded beyond recognition of a liquidity effect. Faster money growth meant more funds for the purchase of bonds, and yields declined.

But experience over the last 10 years has made it clear that further analysis is required. First it is essential to distinguish between money growth that conforms with the Federal Reserve's intentions and that which contravenes them. By this time, nearly everyone knows that too rapid money growth leads to higher short-term interest rates, and unexpectedly slow growth brings lower rates. The interesting case for analysis is the result of a change in the Federal Reserve's money targets.

The initial effects of Federal Reserve efforts to force faster money growth drive short-term interest rates down, as actual growth falls short of the raised target, and the Federal Reserve supplies bank reserves in increased volume. In times before the public became sensitized to inflation, this fall in short rates almost certainly would have been followed by long-term bond rates. Now, that need not happen. People have come to associate faster money growth with faster inflation. So while long-term rates probably fall somewhat, in sympathy with the lower short rates, investors are wary that short-term rates may be only temporarily reduced, and they hesitate before bidding bond yields down very far. The deciding factors will be things like the degree of excess capacity in the economy, and the public's estimate of the central bank's commitment to low inflation. That is why bond rates fall when the Bank of Switzerland announces a lower discount rate, and they rise on the same move by the Bank of England.

The famous Fisher equation illustrates this relationship: $i = r + p^*$, where i, the nominal rate of interest, is expressed in terms of the real rate r and inflationary expectations p^*. The nominal rate i is the rate actually observed in financial markets. Swiss investors still have firm ideas about the long-run inflation rate in their country that are not shaken by temporary changes in monetary policy. When their central bank provides more money, bond prices rise, and the real interest rate falls. British investors cannot have the same confidence. For all they know additional money growth may simply validate a higher inflation rate. The effects on bond prices of monetary expansion are uncertain and so is its impact on the real rate of interest. This relation applies to the Federal Reserve as well and adds to the complexities of its position. For suppose it desires to stimulate the economy and embarks on such a policy. Money stock growth accelerates, and interest rates are initially depressed. But over time, rates may rise in reaction to such a policy; indeed, they may climb above their initial levels. And to the extent that aggregate demand is interest rate sensitive, the policy will not achieve what it set out to.

Other Components of Demand

This returns us to a consideration of the interest rate responsiveness of various measures of spending. Beyond the consumer, described above, are there other sectors that may be susceptible to monetary policy influence?

Business spending on new plant and equipment and on inventories would seem logical possibilities, but the evidence is far from overwhelming. Theoretically, interest rates should be an important determinant of business fixed investment or capital spending, for in one sense they represent the cost of borrowed funds and, in another, they reflect the opportunity cost of reinvesting profits in the business.

However, it would appear that whatever interest rate effects there may be are easily swamped by other factors. As shown in Table 6-7, capacity utilization rates seem to figure very importantly in business investment decisions. This is illustrated by the fact that, as utilization rates get high, capital spending appears to take off.

In addition, business investment in new plant and equipment appears positively related to corporate profits, which provide the wherewithal for some projects and may be a good proxy for business confidence as well. Furthermore, the availability, or shortage, of skilled labor matters, for business may be inclined, or forced, to substitute capital for labor if labor is in tight supply.

Thus, the direct effect of monetary policy on business fixed investment spending would appear to be small at best, and the same statement holds for business spending to accumulate inventories. To be sure, short-term interest rates may play a role in the inventory spending decision, for the stocks have to be financed. But as

TABLE 6-7   Determinants of Capital Spending

(Percent)

	1969	1970	1971	1972	1973	1974	1975	1976	1977	1978
Capacity utilization	88.3	82.5	81.5	87.0	91.8	87.1	73.4	81.1	82.7	85.6
Growth in profits	−5.2	−15.6	19.7	23.3	22.9	11.0	−5.2	30.6	13.3	16.3
Unemployment rate, married males	1.5	2.6	3.2	2.8	2.3	2.7	5.2	4.2	3.6	2.8
Increase in wages	6.6	6.6	7.0	6.4	6.2	7.9	8.4	7.2	7.5	8.0
Capital spending	5.8	−3.8	−1.8	8.1	12.2	−0.3	−13.0	4.8	8.7	8.4
Equipment spending	6.4	−4.4	−1.3	12.1	15.1	3.0	−13.2	5.5	11.6	6.8
Structures spending	4.8	−2.7	−2.6	1.9	7.1	−6.6	−12.7	3.2	2.1	12.3

we have seen in recent years, other influences seem more powerful. Thus, in the high-interest-rate years of 1973–74, inventory spending was strong, even excessive. In retrospect, we know that this was because business executives feared persistent shortages and, in the highly inflationary environment of that time, felt that stocking up would ultimately prove profitable.

On the other hand, interest rates were substantially lower in 1975, and yet inventories were liquidated. Indeed, relatively cautious inventory policies have prevailed since then, despite the fact that major banks would have gladly provided financing at attractive terms.

With business spending relatively insensitive, we are rapidly coming to the end of the list of sectors where "money matters." Certainly, it seems unlikely, to say the least, that Federal Government spending is at all inhibited by monetary policy, or anything else for that matter. For state and local government spending, however, it may be another story. Because some states and localities have legal interest rate ceilings on their borrowing, they cannot go to the tax-exempt bond market when market interest rates are high. This effectively limits their spending, especially on capital projects. Even before legal limits are reached, though, some municipalities may defer borrowing and presumably spending plans in times of high rates, believing that more favorable conditions may be in the offing.

Another relevant factor may be the "Proposition 13 spirit" now alive in the land. In its least sophisticated guise, this spirit represents a rebellion against high state and local taxes, especially property taxes. But in its more sophisticated versions, it reflects a careful weighing of costs and benefits associated with spending plans, with the voters clearly giving the message that they are not prepared to foot the bill for any old scheme that happens to come down the pike. Thus, expensive programs that require financing at high interest rates, and therefore high taxes to service the debt, may not fly as in earlier years.

Moral of the Story

What does all of this amount to? It seems clear that the housing sector—residential construction—is sensitive to monetary policy one way or the other. This is not surprising, for such expenditures are postponable. Hence, monetary ease or restraint can affect the timing of this kind of spending.

But beyond this, the effects of monetary conditions are somewhat diffuse. To be sure, almost every sector is affected to some degree, but it is difficult to identify any area that is substantially altered.

The problem is, though, how does this square with some of the evidence cited earlier, indicating a pervasive, and rapid, reaction of the economy to monetary changes? This is a serious question, and a fully satisfactory answer may not exist at present.

Residential construction is only 4 percent of GNP, not enough to account for a significant response in the overall economy. On the other hand, many other expenditures are tied to housing, including consumer spending on furniture, appliances, and other household items. Similarly, commercial building is related to residential construction, as shopping centers, professional buildings, etc. normally spring up around suburban developments.

Thus, it may be that housing is the leader which pulls at least some other sectors of the economy with it as monetary policy changes. Obviously, employment in construction is directly affected, and this will contribute to a sequence of changes in spending. Public utilities, too, will feel an impact as residential construction swings from boom to bust and back again.

The explanation that is evolving, then, suggests that monetary policy directly influences interest-, and perhaps wealth-, sensitive sectors, principally housing and consumer spending on durable goods. But because other sectors do not compensate completely when housing and closely related areas react to monetary policy changes, there is a multiplier effect, which ultimately affects many areas of the economy, especially business capital spending. It is as if once the initial effects of a monetary policy shift achieve a certain critical mass, the whole economy responds.

The Federal Reserve and Foreign Exchange

From the Teeter-Totter to Fundamentals

Perhaps the most significant change in the monetary policy arena in the past several years has been the attention and emphasis given to the performance of the dollar on foreign exchange markets. In assessing this change, we have to distinguish carefully between two distinctly different types of policy reactions.

Initially, the Federal Reserve was inclined to view the international woes of the dollar as a "teeter-totter" problem. Hence, if the dollar was falling, the problem was that demand for the currency was low relative to supply. Accordingly, the system would jump in on the demand side (buy dollars) to try to stabilize the seesaw.

It became apparent, however, as the problem persisted, that something much more fundamental than short-term steadying of the teeter-totter was needed. Thus, in both 1978 and 1979, the international plight of the currency impinged directly on domestic monetary policy, as the Federal Reserve altered monetary aggregates objectives, interest rate instruments, and even the way policy was implemented in attempts to defend the dollar.

At this point, the jury is still out deliberating the success of the Federal Reserve's efforts. In this chapter, we review recent developments in the international currency markets and what they have meant for domestic markets and policies. In some circles, the trials and tribulations of the dollar abroad are at least occasionally credited, or blamed, for erratic money market and money stock behavior at home. In most cases, these fears appear to be unfounded, for the Federal Reserve's "modus operandi" largely precluded such feedback to the domestic financial scene.

Thus, the exchange value dollar is not the root of all of the nation's economic and financial problems. However, with the international financial system still in a state of flux, if not chaos, we probably have not seen the last of such problems or of dramatic reactions to them.

Dollar Support from the Home Front— Stage One

The U.S. dollar encountered serious problems in the early 1970s, culminating, in two steps, with the Smithsonian agreement of 1971 and the second devaluation and move to floating exchange rate regime in February 1973. The "architects" of this transition were Richard M. Nixon and John Connally, and their policy was one of "benign neglect."

Ironically, in light of its origins in benign neglect, as time has passed it has become clear that for the United States a floating exchange rate regime requires a faster response from its central bank—the Federal Reserve—than was common under fixed rates. This would seem to impose greater monetary discipline on the U.S., since its ability to pursue a policy without regard to international repercussions is constricted. By contrast, a fixed or pegged rate system allows almost indefinite postponement of currency adjustment, a conclusion that should not come as a surprise since controls always involve a slowing in changes that inevitably will occur.

With the advent of flexible exchange rates, a new dimension has been added to monetary policy, and we now have to grapple with a Federal Reserve that has turned increasingly international in its orientation. And, in turn, part of the Federal Reserve's problem may originate in the fact that the U.S. role in world trade has diminished markedly over the past 25 years, thus slowing demand for the dollar as an international currency. As we can see in Figures 7-1 and 7-2, the U.S. share of both world exports and international reserves has dropped steadily in the postwar period. Like it or not, the U.S.

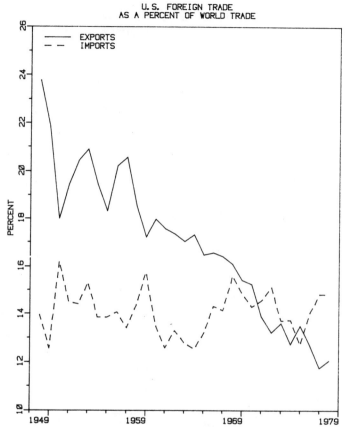

FIGURE 7-1   The U.S. share of world exports has fallen.

appears to be dropping back with the rest of the pack in terms of the magnitude of its role in international transactions.

Another clear indication of how things have gone is illustrated in Figure 7-3, which plots the trade-weighted value of the dollar since 1971, when it was first devalued. Major episodes in recent monetary history are clearly visible.

The dollar basically held its own until early 1973, when accelerating inflation in this country made it all too obvious that the wage and price controls program of the Nixon administration had not permanently reduced inflationary pressures. Accordingly, the dollar was devalued a second time in February 1973, but clearly the situation got worse before it got better. While the U.S. currency bot-

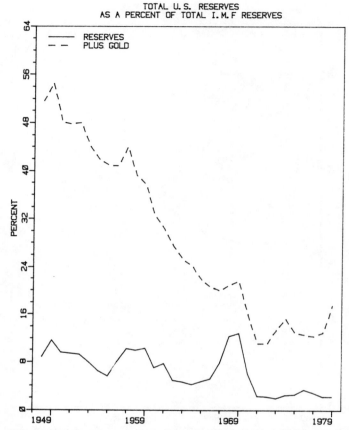

FIGURE 7-2   The United States holds a declining share of world reserve assets.

tomed in the middle of 1973, no real progress was apparent for two years. By mid-1975, however, the dollar was trending up, a move that was sustained, albeit irregularly, until early 1977.

This date marked the high-water mark for the dollar in the post-Smithsonian era. It has been virtually all downhill since then. And of course these exchange rate data reflect dollar support activities conducted by U.S. or foreign monetary authorities over the period.

1978–1979: The Dollar Impinges on Domestic Monetary Policy

As we indicated above, concern over the dollar has reached "record proportions"—if such things can be measured—in the past two

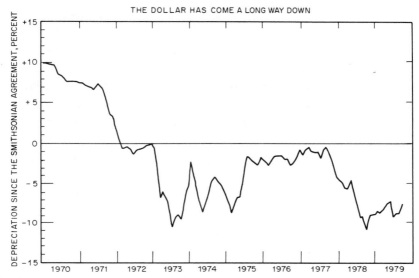

FIGURE 7-3   The fate of the dollar since the Smithsonian agreements.

years, and the Federal Reserve has gone to unprecedented lengths to support the beleaguered currency. The year 1978 started with a bang, as the discount rate was raised ½ percentage point on the first Friday of the year, largely in response to the declining dollar and disorderly foreign exchange market conditions. This move, followed by a ¼ percentage point increase in the System's Federal funds rate objective, caught market participants by surprise even though the Federal Reserve and Treasury had previously announced intentions to use the Exchange Stabilization Fund and swap, or reciprocal currency arrangements, network to actively intervene in the currency markets.

Participants were surprised because prior to this the status of the dollar abroad had never impinged on domestic policy decisions to such an extent. But this episode was just a precursor of developments that were to occur later in the year. In early March, the System bypassed an opportunity to reduce the Federal funds rate even though the monetary aggregates had been far weaker than desired and thus some reduction seemed warranted. Instead, it clung resolutely to the high rate road because of concern over the health of the dollar. Thus, aggregates objectives took a back seat to concerns in the international sphere.

Throughout 1978, the Federal Open Market Committee gave considerable weight in its deliberations to foreign exchange market conditions. Indeed, as early as December 1977, the operating directive adopted by the Federal Open Market Committee stated: "In the conduct of day-to-day operations, account shall be taken of emerging financial market conditions, including the unsettled conditions in foreign exchange markets." In short, it was clear through much of 1978 that the dollar was exerting a major influence on domestic monetary policy, as the Federal Reserve moved well beyond the teeter-totter approach to foreign exchange.

While this trend was underway early, by November 1 it was necessary for the System to take far stronger action. Serious deterioration in the exchange value of the dollar set in around midyear, and matters came to a head in late October, in the wake of the President's anti-inflation program.

The reactions in the exchange markets made it clear that there was no confidence abroad in the measures announced by the President on October 24, and the dollar continued to sink. Finally, on November 1, a major new dollar defense program was unveiled. Its principal tenets were: a dramatic 1 percentage point increase in the discount rate; a rise in reserve requirements on time deposits of $100,000 or more; an increase in the Federal funds to the 9⅝ to 10 percent range, up from 9¼ percent; and several measures to expand the Federal Reserve and Treasury's ability to support the dollar.

Indeed, the authorities made it clear that their objective this time was not just to stabilize the dollar but to correct excessive declines that had already occurred. To accomplish this, substantial foreign exchange market intervention was planned, and accordingly Federal Reserve swap lines (see Table 7-1) with the central banks of West Germany, Japan, and Switzerland were increased materially. Furthermore, the Treasury announced intentions to borrow reserves from the International Monetary Fund, sell foreign-currency-denominated securities (Carter bonds) and special drawing rights (SDRs), and step up gold sales.

If this list sounds incredibly long, it is, for a major effort was undertaken. And it initially was quite successful. It not only contained the tightening of domestic monetary conditions, the corner-

TABLE 7-1   Federal Reserve Reciprocal
Currency Arrangements

Swap Lines

Institution	Amount of facility 1979, $ billions
Austrian National Bank	0.25
National Bank of Belgium	1.00
Bank of Canada	2.00
National Bank of Denmark	0.25
Bank of England	3.00
Bank of France	2.00
German Federal Bank	6.00
Bank of Italy	3.00
Bank of Japan	5.00
Bank of Mexico	0.36
Netherlands Bank	0.50
Bank of Norway	0.25
Bank of Sweden	0.30
Swiss National Bank	4.00
Bank for International Settlements:	
Swiss francs–dollars	0.60
Other authorized European currencies:	
dollars	1.25
Total	29.76

stone of the policy, but also entailed the expansion and activation of the swap lines. Thus, the Federal Reserve jumped on the demand side of the seesaw as well.

Table 7-2 reports Federal Reserve activity in swap transactions over 1978. It is evident that use of the swap lines—which are maintained on a standby basis in any event—shot up dramatically in the fourth quarter, in conjunction with the rescue mission described above. In a swap transaction, one country, say the United States, gains deposits denominated in, say, marks at the Bundesbank in exchange for dollar balances at the New York Federal Reserve. The marks acquired in this fashion can then be used by the Federal Reserve to purchase dollars in the open market or from the Bundesbank, presumably helping to support the currency.

Normally, a swap transaction calls for an initial maturity of three months, after which the line of credit can be liquidated at the orig-

TABLE 7-2   Federal Reserve Drawings and Repayments under Reciprocal Currency Arrangements

Transactions with	Drawings (+) and repayments (−), $ millions			
	1978-I	1978-II	1978-III	1978-IV
German Federal Bank	+1008.5	−800.1	−714.9	−409.7
Bank of Japan	0	0	0	+156.5
Swiss National Bank	+69.0	+4.8	+165.7	+847.5
		−69.0		−231.7
Total	+1077.6	+40.1	+526.5	+5158.2
		−869.1	−741.9	−691.4

inal exchange rate, or renewed. And since foreign central banks actually may have little interest in additional dollar balances, especially in a world where dollars are already in excess supply, the dollars created are usually placed in special, nonnegotiable interest-bearing Treasury certificates of indebtedness.

In essence, a swap transaction represents a loan of currencies between nations. If the mechanism appears unduly complicated and cumbersome, it is because the Federal Reserve Act of 1913, which created the U.S. central bank, did not explicitly allow for direct borrowing of currencies, while swap transactions were permissible.

The first swap line of credit was established on March 1, 1962, between the Federal Reserve and the Bank of France. However, it was not used. Interestingly enough, the first use of swap lines by the United States was actually conducted in Belgian francs and Dutch guilders, not exactly "heavy hitters" in the arena of international finance. This occurred in June 1962, in connection with a "mopping up" of excess dollar balances accumulated by these two central banks.

Dollar Support—Stage Two

The dollar recovered modestly through the first half of 1979, but thereafter it plummeted once again. As a consequence, the Federal Reserve responded in July, August, and September with increases in interest rates at a time when the domestic economy was shaky and the system almost certainly would have preferred to avoid any further tightening action.

Indeed, with the benefit of 20-20 hindsight, it appears that the actions of November 1, 1978, were just the appetizer, and the main course was served, appropriately enough, on Saturday evening, October 6, 1979.

By this time, Paul Volcker had replaced G. William Miller as Chairman of the Federal Reserve. And it was clear that Volcker was inclined to place greater emphasis on the state of the dollar abroad than was Miller and perhaps most of his other predecessors as well. Moreover, by early October, the price of gold had climbed to $440 an ounce, the price of silver had more than doubled in six months, lead and copper prices were up substantially, and speculation was getting underway in even such unlikely commodities as sugar and cocoa.

Faced with the evidence of the incipient stages of a major flight from currencies which could have precipitated a collapse in world trade and a worldwide depression, the Federal Reserve raised the discount rate one percentage point to an unheard of 12 percent, imposed new and increased existing reserve requirements, and announced that henceforth reserves rather than interest rates would serve as the key tool in controlling the monetary aggregates. Thus, deterioration of the dollar prompted a break with techniques carefully constructed by the Federal Reserve over the previous eight or nine years. Shocked market participants had no choice but to take a step back and learn new rules of the game.

It quickly became clear that at least some of the rules were radical departures from the past. The Federal funds rate, which had been tightly controlled by the Federal Reserve and which was trading around 11.75 percent prior to October 6, immediately moved up to a 14–15 percent range, and there were days when transactions occurred in volume at 18 percent and occasionally 20 percent. Short-term Treasury bill yields advanced for a time to over 13 percent, and record high yields were reached on virtually all Government notes and bonds. Almost incredibly, all of this transpired against a very uncertain economic background, with many forecasters feeling that the country was already in a recession.

As of this writing, it remains to be seen whether the Federal Reserve will finally succeed in stemming the tide, thereby stabilizing the dollar. However, even though the story is necessarily unfinished, there are several good reasons for recounting the 1978–1979 episode of "currency chaos." First, it unmistakably illustrates the prominent role international considerations have come to play in U.S. monetary policy deliberations. Certain well-established techniques were ripped unceremoniously from their moorings. Secondly, it highlights some of the more arcane activities in which the Federal Reserve has been engaged in recent years. At this point, it may pay to look at these activities in greater depth.

When the Federal Reserve intervenes in the foreign exchange markets, its trading desk at the New York Bank actually executes orders with dealers in New York. Recent support operations have involved selling marks, Swiss francs, and yen for dollars, the theory being that the demand for dollars is increased at the expense of other currencies. But as shown in Table 7-1, swap lines are in place in many currencies, so presumably operations can be conducted in a wide variety of currencies if appropriate.

Concerted action between central banks is frequently required in exchange market operations. Thus, when the Federal Reserve is active in New York, European central bankers may be selling their currencies for dollars in their markets, and this is true of the Japanese as well. Moreover, if the Federal Reserve really wants to make a "point," it can operate through United States banks with branches abroad to intervene in markets outside of New York. This technique was used, for example, in the crisis days of late October 1978.

Effects on Domestic Financial Markets

Turmoil in the foreign exchange arena feeds back to domestic financial markets and domestic policy operations in a variety of ways. And while these effects can be substantial, they are not usually as disruptive as they are credited with being.

When foreign central banks acquire dollars in the currency markets, they frequently invest these funds in U.S. government securities, often in Treasury bills. Such investment can occasionally lead to a shortage of bills in the domestic market, and bill rates fall relative to yields on other short-term instruments. Indeed, as shown in Table 7-3, foreign official institutions have bought a tremendous

TABLE 7-3   Holdings of U.S. Treasury Debt

($ Billions)

Holder	1973	1974	1975	1976	1977	1978
Total gross public debt	469.9	492.7	576.6	653.5	718.9	789.2
U.S. government agencies and trust funds	129.6	141.2	139.1	147.1	154.8	170.0
Federal Reserve Banks	78.5	80.5	89.8	97.0	102.5	109.6
Commercial banks	60.3	55.6	85.1	103.8	101.4	93.4
National savings banks	2.9	2.5	4.5	5.9	5.9	5.2
Insurance companies	6.4	6.1	9.5	12.7	15.1	15.0
Other corporations	10.9	11.0	20.2	27.7	22.7	20.6
State and local governments	29.2	29.2	34.2	41.6	55.2	68.6
Individuals:						
Savings bonds	60.3	63.4	67.3	72.0	76.7	80.7
Other securities	16.9	21.5	24.0	28.8	28.6	30.0
Foreign and international	55.5	58.4	66.5	78.1	109.6	137.8
Other miscellaneous investors	19.3	23.2	38.0	38.9	46.1	57.4

volume of Treasury debt, both marketable and nonmarketable special issues, in recent years.

If Treasury bills become scarce, the Federal Reserve may have difficulty engaging in the volume of open market operations it desires. For example, for the System to conduct repurchase agreements, government securities dealers must have or be able to obtain collateral—Treasury securities—to provide in exchange for reserves. Thus, if collateral is scarce, the Federal Reserve may be unable to bring the Federal funds rate down to the desired level or, to put it another way, it may be unable to inject the desired quantity of reserves, at least through open market activity.

This is, of course, a technical problem and should not materially hamper monetary policy in the longer run. But market participants cannot always be sure what is intended and what stems from technical problems beyond the System's control. Thus, if the funds rate climbs well above its previous target and remains there for several days or more, concern about a change in policy may heighten. The counterpart of this situation in a regime where bank reserves serve as the instrument of policy would be a surge in bank borrowing from the discount window with nonborrowed reserves in short supply.

This problem is not solely an abstraction. At times in 1978 the funds rate drifted persistently above the Federal Reserve's objective. However, lack of collateral coupled with a desire to show support for the dollar resulted in "tolerance" of a somewhat higher-than-planned Federal funds rate.

The report on open market operations for 1978 states, for example, that as a result of the dollar support package,

> Trading in Federal funds on November 1 jumped immediately to the 9% to 10 percent area—somewhat above the Committee's newly adopted 9½ to 9¾ percent range. In order not to blunt the impact of the dollar defense program, the Desk avoided aggressive action to push the funds rate down to the new range, and trading in funds hovered above 9¾ percent for several days.

Foreigners and Reserves, Money, and Credit

Beginning in early 1978, the System gained the authority to execute foreign account temporary investment orders in the market as customer-related RPs. Such actions have no effect on reserve availability, and hence the Federal Reserve typically passes the orders through to the market when conditions are already about as desired.

On the other hand, direct System transactions with foreign investors do absorb or inject reserves to the banking system. For example, suppose a foreign country acquires dollars in the foreign exchange markets. These dollars are credited to the foreign account at the Federal Reserve and are deducted from member bank reserve accounts. If Government securities are purchased in the market for the foreign account, payment for the securities returns the reserves to the banking system. This is of course true whether the transaction is an outright purchase or a repurchase agreement executed in the market. But if the transaction is conducted only between the System and the foreign account, then the reserves never return to the banking system and, depending on what other operating factors are doing, the market for reserves may tighten, contributing to upward pressure on the Federal funds rate and other short-term interest rates. Similarly, if the Federal Reserve buys securities directly from a foreign account, the operation will add reserves as the dollars are paid out by the account.

From time to time, especially during periods when the dollar is "collapsing" abroad, foreign exchange markets and international capital flows are blamed for conditions in U.S. financial markets. Among the charges frequently levied are that weakness of the dollar contributes to overly rapid domestic money expansion, and that the massive Eurodollar market enables domestic banks to avoid the bite of credit restraint.

In theory, neither of these charges would be true given Federal Reserve operating procedures prior to October 1979. Specifically, when the System targets the Federal funds rate, as it did between 1970 and October 1979, any financial transaction which supplies reserves and puts undesired downward pressure on that rate should be countered by a Federal Reserve response which drains reserves and precludes expansion in money and credit. The importance of this response, automatic when the Federal funds rate is the policy instrument, cannot be overemphasized.

Misconceptions abound on this topic. One of the most persistent, as suggested above, is the view that weakness of the dollar on the currency markets leads to rapid growth in the domestic money supply. The mechanism which purportedly brings this about is borrowing by corporations for the purpose of selling the dollar abroad. If such a plan is implemented, business loans and deposits rise at domestic commercial banks, and these deposits are then sold for foreign currencies. Hence, any initial increase in money is temporary and is now over.

The reserve effect at this point is also "neutral" in the sense that any reserves provided by the System to relieve pressure as deposits rose in the first step have now been "destroyed" as foreign accounts acquired dollars. But foreigners will not hold just dollars—they will turn these in for earning assets. Assuming that they are official accounts and deal directly with the Federal Reserve, the System can execute such orders so that there is no effect on reserves or money.

Even if the reserves somehow return to the banking system,

there will then be downward pressure on the funds rate, prompting the Federal Reserve to step in and absorb funds. Again, the net effect on reserves and deposits is neutral.

Admittedly, the foregoing processes are complicated, and one can easily develop a serious headache trying to follow them. Nevertheless, the major point should be clear. While speculation against the dollar on the part of U.S. corporations can lead to money creation, this will happen only if the Federal Reserve acquiesces and does not absorb reserves when the funds rate signals that such action is appropriate. Furthermore, it is revealing that, while weakness of the dollar has been blamed for rapid money growth, we have never heard anyone maintain that a strong dollar leads to slow money expansion.

The only remaining question, as far as we can see, relates to initial conditions in the banking system: Is the system fully "loaned up" (excess reserves = 0) at the outset? If so, then the expansion in banks' earning assets, the first step in the process, must be supported in some fashion, either by a reduction in other earning assets, say Treasury securities, or by sales of CDs or Eurodollar borrowings. While none of these maneuvers will add to the most common definitions of money, at least two involve expansion in overall bank liabilities. To this extent, then, there could be growth in some liability categories, but not in M-1 or M-2.

In a reserve regime, the crucial factor is whether the Federal Reserve offsets any reserve provision that might occur when foreign accounts purchase financial instruments, say Treasury securities. This may depend on the accuracy of the System's reserve projections, for funds rate signals are not sufficient cause for action in such a regime. However, even if no offset is implemented immediately, data would indicate that reserves are running in excess of targets, the Federal Reserve should take action to correct the problem Once again, then, any increase in the aggregates should be temporary.

To return to the issue that triggered this discussion, we would argue, in fact, that causality is much more likely to run from domestic money growth to the performance of the dollar abroad rather than the reverse. Indeed, over the past several years at least, foreign exchange traders have been both very level-headed and "monetarist" in their assessment of U.S. anti-inflation policies. That is, rhetoric has not counted much with these people, but rather they have monitored domestic money growth, read the inflationary implications of such growth in monetarist terms, and have acted accordingly. Pledges to support the currency and ever-higher domestic interest rates have not succeeded in stabilizing the dollar, for growth in the money stock has not been slowed.

Indeed, the Federal Reserve's struggles with the dollar have prompted some actions it has lived to regret, or at least to reverse. Specifically, in August 1978 reserve requirements were removed from domestic bank borrowings from their foreign branches, thus making it more attractive for banks to borrow funds in the Eurodollar market. Such action was taken to encourage banks to acquire dollars abroad, thus to prop up the demand for dollars. There was probably a lot of straightforward appeal to this idea at the time, given the dollar's problems. In fact, of course, it falls rather neatly, like swap transactions and use of the Exchange Stabilization Fund, into the teeter-totter approach to dollar support.

Unfortunately, a critical side effect of this ostensible cure was that it provided major banks with a nonreservable source of loanable funds. Hence, as credit demands strengthened in 1978 and 1979, banks found they could meet such demand with funds acquired in the Eurodollar market. Partially as a result, monetary restraint was blunted, and the Federal Reserve found itself relying almost exclusively on credit rationing by price, a difficult position to be in in the inflation-charged environment of 1979.

Telltale evidence of the credit ease which prevailed in 1979 despite an avowed policy of restraint is given in Table 7-4, which depicts bank credit expansion over the year. Not only was there rapid expansion in loans, as would be expected, but bank investments in Government and tax-exempt securities also increased.

Normally, when loan demand, especially from business customers, is strong late in an economic expansion, banks find it imperative to sell off significant quantities of fixed income investments, particularly Treasury securities, to acquire loanable funds. The experience in 1966, 1969, and 1974, consistent with this statement,

TABLE 7-4 Bank Credit Expansion

(Percent Change from Preceding Year)

	1966	1969	1974	1979
Total loans and securities	+5.3	+2.9	+9.0	+12.3
Total loans	+7.9	+9.7	+11.4	+14.1
Business loans	+13.1	+12.9	+17.0	+18.3
U.S. Treasury securities	−6.3	−15.7	−7.6	+0.4
Other securities	+8.7	−0.3	+7.6	+11.7

is reported in Table 7-4. However, in 1979 banks were not under pressure to this extent and investments in Treasury and especially municipal securities increased. As the year progressed, it became ever clearer that credit restraint had not yet been achieved in the United States, and turmoil in the foreign exchange and gold markets mounted.

We have described above the currency crisis which erupted in late September and the actions undertaken by the Federal Reserve to stem the tide. One of the System's critical steps was to apply reserve requirements on previously nonreservable sources of funds, including domestic bank borrowings of Eurodollars. Thus, what was deemed a good idea in August 1978 was seen as a mistake in need of correction little more than one year later. But the textbooks tell us that monetary policy is a flexible tool, and the policymakers apparently believe it.

The "Good Old Days"

"Benign neglect" has apparently led to considerable central bank intervention in foreign exchange markets, something its advocates presumably did not foresee. Nevertheless, currency gyrations in the 1970s have been wild, and undoubtedly many central bankers and private market participants long for the more tranquil, fixed exchanged rate days of yore. But currency crises are nothing new— only the names of the players and orders of magnitude have changed.

The fixed exchange rate regime which came out of the Bretton Woods agreements of 1944 was in reality a pegged rate system. In this system, a government, say the United Kingdom, undertook to maintain the value of its currency in a narrow 1 percent range in relation to the dollar. For example, if the agreed-upon exchange rate were £1 = $2.40, then the Bank of England would intervene if sterling fell below $2.38 or rose above $2.42.

To accomplish this pegging, the British authorities would need an exchange stabilization fund consisting of dollars, other foreign currencies, and possibly gold. Furthermore, as part of Bretton Woods, the International Monetary Fund (IMF) was created, and the Fund provided facilities for currency borrowing by its members. While in fact the lending operations of the IMF are technically sales of currencies, the important point is that sources of foreign currencies beyond their own holdings were available to IMF members. Moreover, until 1971, the United States maintained convertibility of dollars for gold, so that countries with an excess of dollars or those with a yen for gold and access to dollars could obtain gold from the United States if push came to shove.

Bretton Woods, and variations on that theme, basically established a multitiered approach to exchange rate parity. Rates were to be pegged, except where long-term fundamental balance of payments disequilibria required revaluations. To maintain the parities, there was each country's own stabilization fund, access to the resources of the IMF, the growing Federal Reserve swap network, and gold.

As if this weren't enough, and it apparently wasn't, SDRs or Special Drawing Rights, were also created by IMF members as a new reserve asset. SDRs, sometimes referred to as "paper gold," can be used to settle balance of payments gaps or to acquire foreign exchange. While SDRs are created by the IMF, a country's use of its allocation involves a reconstitution provision, to avoid large and persistent payments deficits financed continuously by SDRs.

Despite all the provisions and wrinkles, the fixed exchange rate system came toppling down in the early 1970s. And even before its fatality, there were signs of very serious cracks in the system.

One major crisis in the "good old days" began in late 1967. In November of that year, the pound sterling was devalued, but only after the mighty effort which had been mounted to avoid such action had failed. Whatever the long-run benefits to Britain, and they were probably substantial, the devaluation certainly did not calm the markets in the short run. Instead, the demand for gold surged, confidence in virtually all currencies diminished, and sterling in particular was "pounded." A full-fledged crisis was present and accounted for by March 1968.

To remedy the situation, the central banks of most major countries terminated official intervention in private gold markets, thus abandoning the commitment to hold the price of gold at $35 an ounce, except for transfers among monetary authorities. And swap lines were increased, so that the Bank of England got a total of $4 billion for the defense of sterling. The Federal Reserve, too, increased its lines of credit, by nearly $1.8 billion, to the then impressive total of $9.4 billion.

Does all this sound familiar? It should, for more than 10 years later a similar series of events, although focused on the dollar, was being replayed. And the question may be asked: why, despite valiant efforts by central bankers and changes in exchange rate regimes, do such crises recur? More directly why haven't persistent increases in domestic interest rates succeeded in improving the trade balance and in arresting the decline in the dollar?

At least in part, the answer appears to be founded on monetarist teachings. Higher interest rates in the United States than in other major countries should normally encourage capital flows into this country and a concomitant rise in the relative demand for dollars on currency markets. This effect should occur provided that the expected foreign exchange value of the dollar does not decline so rapidly as to offset the positive advantage implied by interest rate differentials.

But this is precisely what appears to have happened in recent years. Nominal interest rates in the United States have climbed dramatically higher, but at the same time money growth has accelerated. And with the acceleration, the expected future value of the dollar relative to foreign currencies has plummeted, wiping out the interest rate differential.

High interest rates and a steadily declining dollar seem to have led to little convincing improvement in the trade balance. Of course, theory suggests that high interest rates will cut into interest-sensitive spending components, thereby slowing aggregate demand, including the demand for imported goods. And the drop in the dollar should make U.S. exports more attractive while reducing demand for imports. Nevertheless, in recent years the United States has consistently run up foreign trade deficits.

These disappointing results appear to be a classic case of the "real world" being in fact far more complicated than the theory. For example, a declining dollar should decrease the demand for imported goods, but this effect can be mitigated to a considerable extent if the price effect of the change in currency values is not fully passed through by foreign manufacturers. To be sure, profit margins will erode in the short run, but this strategy could still be in the foreign manufacturers' long-run interest, provided they can maintain or improve market share.

Of course, the huge increase in oil prices—where demand is inelastic—has served to maintain an unfavorable trade balance, but many other industrial countries have run into this problem. There may be, though, export subsidies provided by foreign governments which would exacerbate the U.S. trade gap. And there are cases of "dumping" which go beyond economics to the political arena.

On the demand side, it is probably true that the price sensitivity or "elasticity" of demand for U.S. exports is not very high. Thus, when the dollar falls in value, demand for U.S. goods abroad does not expand significantly. Sales of major exported goods—high-technology products like computers, agricultural products, and commercial aircraft—just are not stimulated substantially by relative price declines.

Indeed, it is possible that as the dollar depreciates, the U.S. payments deficit deteriorates further, so that equilibrium is not reestablished by the market left to its own devices. This kind of instability would create real problems for the self-adjustment mechanism of a flexible exchange rate regime, necessitating intervention by the authorities.

Can Monetary Policy Go it Alone?

It may be asking too much of monetary policy to simultaneously achieve exchange rate stability and domestic objectives like full employment. Obviously, in certain situations these goals may conflict: for example, stabilization of the exchange value of the dollar may require a slowing of money growth, while reducing unemployment may require just the reverse.

But more broadly, there is a very real question about the U.S. commitment to the kinds of anti-inflation policies necessary to rebuild international confidence in the currency. Under these circumstances, it would seem essential to get the monetary authorities some help, and the logical source, at least on the demand management side, is fiscal policy. Here, in recent years, the record has been rather miserable. Figures on Federal spending and tax revenues are presented in Table 7-5. Over the past ten years, through 1979, the Federal budget has been in uninterrupted deficit, with the gap ranging from about $3 to $66 billion. On average, the deficit has been about $30 billion.

In some respects, these figures are not surprising, especially given the size of the U.S. economy. But note that a surplus was not even achieved after several consecutive years of economic expansion; the closest the country came was in fiscal 1974—a deficit of $4.7 billion.

TABLE 7-5   Federal Budget
($ Billions)

Fiscal year	Budget receipts	Budget outlays	Surplus (+) or deficit (−)
1965	116.8	118.4	−1.6
1966	130.9	134.7	−3.8
1967	149.6	158.3	−8.7
1968	153.7	178.8	−25.2
1969	187.8	184.5	+3.2
1970	193.7	196.6	−2.8
1971	188.4	211.4	−23.0
1972	208.6	232.0	−23.4
1973	232.2	247.1	−14.8
1974	264.9	269.6	−4.7
1975	281.0	326.2	−45.2
1976	300.0	366.4	−66.4
TQ	81.8	94.7	−13.0
1977	357.8	402.7	−45.0
1978	402.0	450.8	−48.8
1979	465.9	493.6	−27.7

What this depicts, in short, is a fundamental reluctance to limit the growth in Federal spending in any meaningful way. This record of persistent deficits is incredible in view of the revenue generating capability of the U.S. tax system, particularly in inflationary times. To be sure, this problem is widely recognized, and thus may be one principal reason why U.S. anti-inflation programs lack credibility. If so, it helps to explain the unending troubles of the dollar abroad.

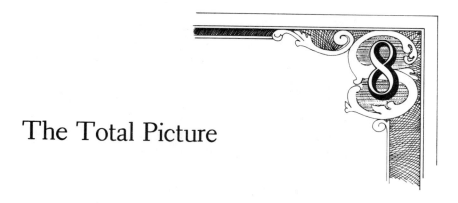

The Total Picture

Introduction

By now, we should recognize that familiar statements like "the Federal Reserve today raised interest rates by ½ percentage point," or "commercial banks start an upward rate spiral by boosting the prime rate" convey a kernel of truth, but give a misleading impression of how interest rates are determined. As powerful as the Federal Reserve is, it does not control interest rates irrespective of developments in the private sector of the economy. And while the banks are a very important component of the financial system, they cannot establish rates without regard to the overall supply and demand for credit.

Indeed, much of this book has been devoted to examination of the complex interrelationships in financial markets that contribute both to Federal Reserve policy decisions and to interest rate movements. In this final chapter, we draw upon our previous discussion to provide an overview of the major factors that go into interest rate determination. Among the factors we consider in addition to the Federal Reserve and the banking system are fundamental credit demands, inflationary expectations, financial innovation, and concerns with credit quality or risk.

Dominance of Economic Fundamentals

By varying the supply of reserves available to the banking system, the Federal Reserve can normally keep the Federal funds rate within desired limits, at least in the short run. And this control extends directly to rates on other short-term instruments—like CDs, commercial paper, Treasury bills—since these instruments are close substitutes and a change in the funds rate will affect the return on all of them.

But once we move beyond short-run control of short-term interest rates, we find that the Federal Reserve faces a much more difficult task. Essentially, this is because economic fundamentals have a way of asserting themselves in the long run.

To see this, suppose that the economy is booming and credit demand is growing rapidly. In this environment, interest rates would be expected to rise, as demand for financing outpaces supply at prevailing interest rate levels. The Federal Reserve, if it chooses to do so, can prevent this increase in the short run by expanding the supply of reserves sufficiently.

In the longer run, however, it is highly unlikely that stability can be maintained at interest rate r_0 (see Figure 8-1). For a booming economy will ultimately generate inflationary pressures which, if the Federal Reserve is doing its job, it will have to resist by permitting, or encouraging, rates to climb. Thus, the economic fundamentals dominate interest rate determination in the long term.

Surpluses and Deficits

While there are obviously a multitude of interest rates, they all reflect the cost of obtaining money to the borrower and a return on invested funds to the lender. And since people or firms do not bor-

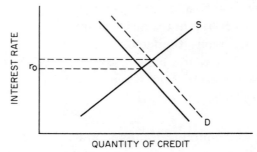

FIGURE 8-1   Supply and demand of credit.

row for their health, but because they have spending plans they want to carry out which exceed current income, the "real" or spending side of the economy is critical in establishing interest rates levels.

Similarly, lenders have income which exceeds their immediate needs—they have a surplus. That is, their participation in the income-expenditure side of the economy has generated funds which they are willing to lend, at a price.

So the picture which emerges is, in a nutshell: interest rates are influenced simultaneously by spending activity, by economic units' preferences for holding certain financial assets or issuing specific types of liabilities, and by Federal Reserve objectives for the performance of the economy. This book has focused heavily on the role of the Federal Reserve, but it is also essential to look at the other factors determining interest rates.

Initial Equilibrium

If the economy is growing at a steady 3.5 percent per year, and the funds available for lending by surplus units equal the deficits of borrowing units, then as a first approximation interest rates should be stable. In Table 8-1, we display the positions of major surplus and deficit sectors in 1964, as close to a period of interest rate stability as we can find in recent history.

By definition, aggregate surpluses have to equal deficits, so there

TABLE 8-1   Surplus or Deficit of Major Sectors of the Economy, 1964

($ Billions)

	Surplus	Deficit
Household	24.1	
Nonfinancial business		14.8
State and local government		3.0
U.S. Government		3.3
Federal Reserve and government agencies		0.3
Rest of world		4.8
Financial intermediaries	3.0	
Discrepancy		0.9
Totals	27.1	27.1

is nothing surprising about the data in the table. What is important, however, is the fact that at these values, intended lending is equal to desired borrowing, so there is no pressure for interest rates to change. This stability in rates can in theory last indefinitely. However, several things may disturb the situation, including OPEC oil price increases, labor strikes, or significant changes in agricultural price supports.

In addition to these "outside shocks," the equilibrium may be disturbed by developments within the economy itself. For example, suppose that business executives become "euphoric" and embark on a capital spending boom. To finance investment in plant and equipment, business firms step up their borrowing. But as there has not been a commensurate increase in the surplus of lending units, the demand for funds will exceed supply, placing upward pressure on interest rates since rates represent the price of money. This is equivalent, in Table 8-1, to an increase in the nonfinancial corporate sector's deficit without a concomitant expansion in another unit's surplus or diminution in another deficit. There is adjustment, however, for as rates rise, some potential borrowers are discouraged, as lower-yielding investment projects are postponed or canceled. At the same time, higher rates persuade some units to postpone consumption and save income instead, thereby adding to the supply of loanable funds. Ultimately, a new equilibrium is established, but at generally higher interest rates.

A similar scenario may ensue if, say, consumption spending surges, because consumers become concerned about future inflation. Should a "buy now" psychology take hold, household saving would diminish but there would be no comparable decrease in credit demands. As a result, demand for credit would once again exceed supply, leading to upward pressure on interest rates. As rates climb, a new equilibrium would be established, as in our previous example.

In Table 8-2 surpluses and deficits in recent years are depicted. Obviously, there are wide swings in the role of the major sectors in each year, as personal savings rates change, profits and internal cash generation vary, and government budgets swing from surplus to deficit.

TABLE 8-2 Surpluses and Deficits in Recent Years

($ Billions)

Sector	1973		1974		1975		1976		1977		1978		1979	
	Surplus	Deficit	Surplus	Deficit	Surplus	Deficit	Surplus	Deficit	Surplus	Deficit	Surplus	Deficit	Surplus	Deficit
Household	66.7		75.7		101.6		90.4		73.8		81.9		78.8	
Nonfinancial business		71.7		72.5		8.9		38.6		61.3		75.7		89.1
State and Local Governments	1.4			7.7		12.7	4.3		3.6		0.5			0.1
U.S. Government		7.4		6.0		73.6		57.8		54.0		34.7		17.7
Federal Reserve and government agencies	0.5		0.7		0.8		0.6		0.9		1.7		1.4	
Rest of world	2.8		4.2			17.1		8.8	20.9		12.7			9.0
Financial intermediaries	8.1		7.3		6.7		9.8		14.2		16.7		18.7	
Discrepancy		0.4		1.7	3.2		8.7		1.9			3.1		17.0
Totals	79.5	79.5	87.9	87.9	112.3	112.3	109.5	109.5	115.3	115.3	113.5	113.5	115.9	115.9

Note that, over the period depicted here, the deficit of the business sector varied between $9 and $75 billion, and the Federal government similarly had a very wide range of financial requirements. Meantime, the household sector's surplus ran between $66 and $105 billion.

Among other things, Table 8-2 shows how "crowding out" at least potentially might occur. For any rise in the Federal government deficit must be offset by either an enlarged surplus or a reduced deficit elsewhere. Hence, consumer or business spending could be held below what otherwise would occur by government activity, as the adjustments described above work themselves out.

Federal Reserve Policy Response

As discussed above, developments in the real economy can influence interest rates well apart from any actions by the Federal Reserve. And in a dynamic economy like ours, such developments are not at all unusual. Of course, the Federal Reserve can try to offset the kind of pressures described here, and in the short run it may be successful. But in the longer run, such success is largely self-defeating.

Perhaps one of the thorniest problems faced by the Federal Reserve, at least since the mid-1960s, is the existence and persistence of inflationary expectations. Such expectations are largely unobservable, but there is nevertheless no question of their significance.

Inflationary expectations affect interest rates in a variety of ways. From the lenders' point of view, higher nominal returns will be demanded since it is expected that inflation will erode the value of interest income over time. And while borrowers certainly prefer low rates, if they anticipate inflation they know they can repay their debts in depreciated dollars. Thus, they will not be easily discouraged by interest rate increases.

Inflationary expectations complicate the Federal Reserve's job in several respects. For one thing, the existence of such expectations means that the System can never be completely confident that, if it wants to pursue restraint, it has achieved "high" interest rates. Perhaps more importantly, expectations are undoubtedly formed on the basis of what is happening in the economy. Hence, the Federal Reserve may frequently find itself struggling to establish rates which are incompatible with prevailing expectations.

As a first approximation, expectations may be formed on the basis of past price behavior. This model of expectations formation is known as "adaptive" expectations. It says that the inflation people expect today depends on the rates of price increase experienced in the recent past. Thus, if inflation over the past four or five years ran in a range of, say, 4–6 percent per annum, then there is a good possibility that this is the kind of price performance now anticipated.

Rational Expectations

Since the early 1970s, actual price behavior has been highly volatile, and the adaptive expectations approach is probably no longer appropriate. Instead, expectations of future inflation may be formed in a more sophisticated, or "rational," way.

Rational expectations assume that participants look at much more than the previous path of prices in forming a "judgment" on the future. In particular, people have learned that prices are influenced by a host of variables, including growth in the monetary aggregates, the state of the Federal budget, governmental agricultural and labor policies, industrial capacity relative to output, and possibly other factors as well.

There is obviously much to consider, but in an environment of rapid inflation those who correctly anticipate it will be amply rewarded. But note that inflationary expectations—and especially rational expectations—complicate the job of the Federal Reserve considerably. To see this, suppose the Federal Reserve wants to lower interest rates to stimulate the economy. It can begin by adding reserves to the banking system through open market purchases, thereby putting downward pressure on the Federal funds rate. But it is entirely possible that economic units will recognize this stimulative policy and fear the future inflationary consequences of it. If they do, long-term interest rates could rise rather than fall, as the Federal Reserve intends.

An ever more graphic example of this occurs if people are at least somewhat monetarist in their views. In this case, if the System embarks on an expansionary policy which lowers the funds rate and/or boosts the money supply, expectations of higher prices will almost automatically be triggered. Again, the Federal Reserve will find itself thwarted insofar as a reduction in longer-term yields is concerned.

Quality and Supply Factors

There are other factors which influence interest rates from time to time, some of which aid the Federal Reserve and some which add to the complexities of its job. For example, the relative supply of alternative types of issues may affect the interest rate spreads between these instruments. Thus, if the Federal government is running a large deficit while, at the same time, private borrowers are hesitant or cautious, returns on government securities should rise relative to those on private instruments. But if the dollar is declining abroad and foreign central banks are acquiring the U.S. currency in exchange for their own, they may buy a substantial volume of government securities and preclude the anticipated rate movement.

Quality spreads also typically vary with business conditions. Normally, as an economic expansion continues and confidence rises, interest rate spreads between different quality issues diminish. Thus, the rate differential between, say, triple-A and triple-B rated corporate bonds declines because investors do not fear default by the lower-quality issuer.

However, late in an expansion or early in the ensuing recession, quality spreads start to widen out. This happens because investors reevaluate the risks associated with alternative issues under deteriorating economic conditions and typically require greater compensation to hold the riskier bond. Frequently in a downturn, there will be some prominent casualties—Penn Central, the REITs, Franklin National Bank, New York City—which will make investors particularly quality conscious. It may become virtually impossible for some borrowers to tap the bond market under these conditions, at least at rates that they find acceptable. This, of course, adds further to financial pressures.

At such times, the Federal Reserve may step in to try to calm unsettled markets. Limitations on discount window borrowing may be relaxed, so that banks can gain reserves to lend to customers encountering difficulty in rolling over obligations. The prime example of this, at least in recent years, occurred during the collapse of the Penn Central Transportation Company, in the spring of 1970. In this case, the System assured banks that funds would be available for worthy borrowers.

When the real estate investment trusts (REITs) were threatened with insolvency in 1974–75, the Federal Reserve applied "moral suasion." This term means that the System suggested politely to friendly bankers that they keep the REITs afloat wherever possible. To be sure, some REITs collapsed in bankruptcy, but many survived, and a financial panic, which a succession of bankruptcies would have triggered, was avoided.

The Record

While all these crosscurrents in the financial system and economy are real enough, the Federal Reserve is "paid" to deal with them and still accomplish its objectives. And the bottom line is: How well has the Federal Reserve succeeded in controlling the monetary aggregates? Since the System sets the targets itself, results would seem to be biased in its favor.

Nevertheless, as shown in Table 8-3, the results to date have not been very exciting. Money growth has varied sharply from year to

TABLE 8-3 Growth in the Monetary Aggregates

(Percent)

Year	M-1	M-2	M-3
1970	5.1	8.0	8.1
1971	6.5	11.4	13.5
1972	9.1	11.3	13.3
1973	6.0	8.8	8.8
1974	4.7	7.2	6.7
1975	4.3	8.6	11.4
1976	6.2	11.4	13.1
1977	7.9	9.3	11.2
1978	6.7	8.3	9.2
1979	5.7	8.4	8.0

year, and the Federal Reserve has rather frequently missed its objectives for growth in the monetary aggregates. Errors were particularly serious in 1972, 1977, and 1978.

In 1972, the domestic economy was enjoying its second full year of expansion following the 1969–1970 recession. It was clearly a time for the Federal Reserve to keep growth in the monetary aggregates from accelerating or decelerating sharply, since there was no reason to further stimulate the economy nor to try to abort the recovery.

As it turned out, however, expansion in the money stock measures jumped significantly. Some have attributed this result to the fact that Arthur Burns, who was Chairman of the Federal Reserve Board at the time, was trying to help Richard Nixon gain reelection. Others consider it an honest mistake. However this may be, it proved to be costly, for the subsequent acceleration of inflation and worldwide commodity boom can be at least partially attributed to it.

It appears that this error may have been repeated in 1977–1978, when the money supply, particularly M-1, ran well above the System's expressed targets (see Table 8-4). Undoubtedly, part of the

TABLE 8-4   Growth Targets for the Monetary Aggregate
(Percent)

Period	Month established	M-1	Actual	M-2	Actual	M-3	Actual
March 1975–March 1976	April 1975	5–7½	5.3	8½–10½	9.7	10–12	12.3
June 1975–June 1976	June 1975	5–7½	4.4	8½–10½	8.8	10–12	11.3
1975-II–1976-II	July 1975	5–7½	5.4	8½–10½	9.6	10–12	12.0
1975-III–1976-III	Oct. 1975	5–7½	4.6	7½–10½	9.3	9–12	11.5
1975-IV–1976-IV	Jan. 1976	4½–7½	5.8	7½–10½	10.9	9–12	12.7
1976-I–1977-I	April 1976	4½–7	6.5	7½–10	11.0	9–12	12.8
1976-II–1977-II	July 1976	4½–7	6.8	7½–9½	10.8	9–11	12.5
1976-III–1977-III	Nov. 1976	4½–6½	8.0	7½–10	11.1	9–11½	12.7
1976-IV–1977-IV	Jan. 1977	4½–6½	7.9	7–10	9.8	8½–11½	11.7
1977-I–1978-I	April 1977	4½–6½	7.7	7–9½	8.8	8½–11	10.5
1977-II–1978-II	July 1977	4–6½	8.2	7–9½	8.6	8½–11	10.0
1977-III–1978-III	Oct. 1977	4–6½	8.1	6½–9	8.6	8½–10½	9.6
1977-IV–1978-IV	Feb. 1978	4–6½	7.3	6½–9	8.5	7½–10	9.4
1978-I–1979-I	April 1978	4–6½	5.1	6½–9	7.6	7½–10	8.7
1978-II–1979-II	July 1978	4–6½	4.8	6½–9	7.7	7½–10	8.6
1978-III–1979-III	Oct. 1978	2–6	5.2	6½–9	8.2	7½–10	8.6
1978-IV–1979-IV	Feb. 1979	1½–4½	5.4	5–8	8.5	6–9	8.2

problem in this case was that the Federal Reserve simply underestimated the ongoing strength of the economic expansion. That is, it failed to locate the liquidity preference schedule accurately. This does not excuse, however, the System's persistent failure to correct the error once it was obvious to all.

There are at least four reasons why the Federal Reserve may significantly miss its money supply targets.

1. Its forecast of the economy may be poor, so that it seriously over- (or under-) estimates the strength of the economy and therefore of money demand.

2. Random shocks, like a quadrupling of oil prices, a major strike, or the imposition of wage-price controls, can disrupt normal economic processes and cause the System to lose its bearings.

3. The Federal Reserve may overestimate (or underestimate) the response of money growth to changes in interest rates or in bank reserves, so that it is mistaken about the effects of its own actions.

4. The preceding problem may be further aggravated in a world of financial innovation and sophisticated liability and asset management, for "hot money" will flow to the instrument providing the best return, perhaps affecting the monetary aggregates appreciably.

Of those listed above, the most serious problems are probably (3) and (4), for they affect the System's performance directly. Little can be done about random shocks (2) except to try to ride them out. And in any event, they probably represent periods when the money stock measures are not very useful as intermediate policy targets or as indicators. As to forecasting ability (1), the Federal Reserve is not infallible, but it devotes considerable resources to the effort, and is probably at least as good as anybody in government.

But what is the response of the money supply to changes in interest rates and in reserves? Until recently, it was the Federal funds rate that the System controlled most directly—that served as the operating instrument of policy. The empirical evidence on this topic indicated a response such that if the Federal funds rate rises 1 percentage point, say, from 7 to 8 percent, the money supply (M-1) should fall 4.5 percent, or about $17 billion at current levels, all other things equal. The comparable response for M-2 is 5.0 percent, or a decline of $47 billion, if the System boosts the funds rate 1 percentage point. The responses described above do not occur instantaneously, however. In fact, most estimates suggest that it takes six to eight months for the full impact of a change in the Federal funds rate to be felt on the money stock measures. This means, of course, that even if the economy were flat, several months would be required before the impact of policy could be discerned. If the economy is growing, the lag is presumably the same, but it may be more difficult—both for policymakers and outside analysts alike— to tell what is going on.

With the change in policy regimes in late 1979 to emphasis on bank reserves, the money-reserve connection, of course, becomes paramount. But because of the newness of the approach, there is not a wealth of evidence on how this policy mechanism works. This is particularly true since any estimates that are available are based on earlier policy regimes that are no longer appropriate.

Be that as it may, statistics relating nonborrowed reserves to the money stock indicate that, at current levels of M-1 of $380 billion and of $42 billion for reserves, a $1 billion increase in nonborrowed reserves will be associated with a $3.5 billion gain in M-1, again assuming other things equal. This will probably take six to eight months to fully work itself out. The corresponding "response elasticity" for M-2 appears to be about $9 billion. These figures at least give the Federal Reserve a handle on how its current actions affect its intermediate objectives—M-1 and M-2—until further experience and evidence are accumulated.

Financial Innovation

Recently, control of the conventional monetary aggregates has been complicated by a proliferation of new money market instruments. Most notable among these, perhaps, are the six-month money market certificates offered by thrift institutions and commercial banks. For a time, thrifts could pay ¼ percentage point more on such accounts than was available on six-month Treasury bills. This feature enabled the thrifts to attract a substantial volume of "hot money"—money that flows to the highest available return—that they would otherwise have lost.

The six-month money market certificates were the first financial innovation that really enabled thrift institutions to compete effectively for short-term deposits with banks and money market instruments. Our estimates indicate that, beginning in June 1978 and continuing through March 1978, thrift deposits grew much more rapidly than would have been predicted on the basis of historical experience during periods of high interest rates. This success can be attributed to the money market certificates.

Since time and savings accounts at thrift institutions are included in M-3, but not in narrower definitions of money, this aggregate gained at the expense of M-1 and M-2. The interest rate differential between thrifts and Treasury bills was partially eliminated in March 1979, however, so we may see a return to more typical relations between the aggregates.

The past few years have witnessed other developments which have altered the financial structure as well. The development of NOW (negotiable order of withdrawal) in New England, and now in New York State, allows banks and thrifts to pay interest on checking accounts, further blurring the distinction between types of deposits and depository institutions. Automatic transfer accounts (ATs), which allow funds to move automatically from savings to checking accounts to cover checks as they are presented, make it easy for households and other units to economize on demand deposits.

In sum, the innovations described above have cut materially into the usefulness of M-1 as an intermediate policy target. It has simply become very easy to keep M-1 balances to a minimum, and there is little known with confidence about reported M-1 in relation to GNP. Another very important development has been the growth and increasing flexibility of the money market mutual funds. These funds, designed for both small corporations and individuals, pool money and invest in high-yielding short-term instruments—domestic CDs, commercial paper, bankers' acceptances, Eurodollar CDs.

There is little question but that, in periods of high interest rates, these funds attract interest-sensitive money at the expense of demand and time and savings accounts. Moreover, since many money market funds now offer check-writing privileges, they are good substitutes for transactions balances.

Table 8-5 provides an idea of the volume of funds involved in these instruments. It is apparent that there have been marked increases in the popularity of such vehicles, as interest rate levels have trended up. This is not surprising, for rates represent the "opportunity cost" of holding demand deposits, i.e., the interest forgone by keeping assets in *M*-1.

Effects on Velocity

As a result of these innovations—and there will undoubtedly be more to follow—traditional distinctions between financial assets have diminished. Hence, in pursuing money supply targets, the Federal Reserve faces both a definitional problem and the problem that the object of its strategy is constantly shifting.

These difficulties became particularly pronounced in the latter part of 1978 and in early 1979. Shown in Table 8-6 are growth in the aggregates, in GNP, and the implied change in velocity in the 1970s. It is evident that, for *M*-1 through *M*-3, velocity increased as the period progressed. For *M*-1, in particular, it accelerated to almost astronomical proportions at times in 1978 and in early 1979. This reflects, of course, the evolution of a myriad of close substitutes for demand deposits.

It is equally interesting to note that *M*-4, which adds large negotiable CDs issued by commercial banks to *M*-2, on average dis-

TABLE 8-5   Money Market Certificates at Thrifts and Money Market Mutual Fund Shares

($ Billions)

Period		Money market mutual fund shares	Money market certificates at S&Ls	Money market certificates at MSBs
1978:	I	+1.7		
	II	+1.3	+5.4	+2.0
	III	+1.4	+13.9	+4.4
	IV	+2.4	+23.4	+6.6
1979:	I	+7.2	+30.4	+8.5
	II	+7.9	+27.5	+2.9
	III	+8.3	+14.3	+3.9
	IV	+11.0	+25.1	+6.0

TABLE 8-6   Growth in GNP, Monetary Aggregates, and Velocity
(Annual Percentage Changes)

	GNP Growth	M-1 Growth	V-1 Growth	M-2 Growth	V-2 Growth	M-3 Growth	V-3 Growth
1971	8.2	6.6	1.6	11.3	−3.1	13.5	−5.3
1972	10.1	8.4	1.7	11.2	−1.1	13.3	−3.2
1973	11.6	6.2	5.4	8.8	2.8	9.0	2.6
1974	8.1	5.1	3.0	7.7	0.4	7.1	1.0
1975	8.2	4.6	3.6	8.4	−0.2	11.1	−2.9
1976	11.3	5.8	5.5	10.9	0.4	12.7	−1.4
1977	11.6	7.9	3.7	9.8	1.8	11.7	−0.1
1978	12.0	7.3	4.7	8.5	3.5	9.4	2.6
1979	11.3	4.8	6.5	7.4	3.9	8.2	3.1

played more stability in relation to GNP than the other aggregates. This would seem reflective of bank liability management practices, for as growth in other deposit sources slow, commercial banks can market negotiable CDs more aggressively, thereby using this instrument to take up the slack.

Other Policy Objectives

As we have previously emphasized, the monetary aggregates are not the be all and end all of Federal Reserve policy. The authorities frequently look beyond the money supply to developments in the economy itself. Occasionally, they have multiple objectives, which might involve, say, trying to stimulate business spending on new plant and equipment while simultaneously trying to slow other components of aggregate demand.

A classic example of this type of strategy is known as Operation Twist, a policy actively pursued back in the 1960s and considered from time to time since then. Operation Twist was essentially an attempt to influence the shape of the yield curve—the term structure of interest rates, or the relation between yield to maturity and the length of time to maturity of a reasonably homogeneous group of securities—by buying some maturities of government securities while selling others. The underlying idea was that, by influencing relative supply and demand in the bond markets, predictable changes in interest rates could be brought about. More specifically, the idea was to purchase long-term government bonds, thus helping to put a lid on longer-term interest rates. Keeping long-term rates relatively low was viewed as aiding capital expansion in this country. At the same time, the Federal Reserve would sell Treasury bills, thus putting a floor under short-term rates. In this way, the yield curve was to be twisted, so that its traditional upward slope was reduced or eliminated.

For this policy to be successful, the money and bond markets have to be at least somewhat segmented. The term "segmented" means that relative supply and demand in specific sectors of the market—short-, intermediate-, or long-term—influence rates in that sector irrespective of what is happening elsewhere.

As opposed to this view of the markets, many analysts hold to an expectational or expectational-cum-liquidity preference model. According to this approach, the shape of the yield curve is determined by borrowers' and lenders' expectations concerning future interest rate movements, with perhaps the concept of liquidity preference appended.

So, for example, suppose interest rates were generally expected to rise. Then borrowers would currently prefer to issue long-term obligations and lock up today's relatively low rates. But lenders would want to make only short-term commitments, postponing long-term advances until interest rates climbed.

With lenders preferring the short end and borrowers the long-term area, the yield curve would be upward-sloping. This slope, which is typical, could also be fostered by lenders' preference for more liquid, short-term debt, which means that they must be paid a premium to lend for longer periods of time.

Operation Twist can work if markets are segmented, but it will be unsuccessful if there is close substitution between maturities and the expectational theory holds, unless expectations can be influenced. As it turned out, it appears that the operation was unsuccessful in the early 1960s, in that the Federal Reserve was unable to alter the yield curve in the desired direction.

The motivation behind this attempt at yield curve manipulation is instructive, however. Not only did the Federal Reserve want to create an environment favorable to capital spending, but it also wanted to try to attract short-term financial capital into this country to offset the chronic balance of trade deficit. Hence, high short-term rates were to bring funds in from overseas, while long-term rates were to be kept low enough to stimulate plant and equipment outlays.

In short, the Federal Reserve embarked on this strategy because it had dual policy objectives—one domestic and one international. And since the early 1960s, developments abroad have increasingly intruded on the consciousness of the policymakers.

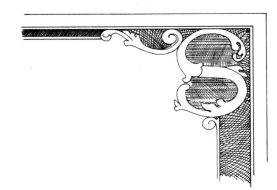

Glossary

Banker's Acceptance   A draft drawn on a bank ordering the bank to pay a particular sum to a specified party at a specified future date. Under a prearranged agreement these drafts are "accepted" by banks, indicating willingness to make such payments at the stated time.

Carter Bonds   Foreign-currency-denominated obligations of the U.S. Treasury sold in several major European countries in 1978 and 1979.

Certificates of Deposit (CDs)   Commercial bank liabilities issued in denominations of $100,000 or more with a specified maturity and paying a market rate of return. There is a very active and well-developed secondary market in such instruments.

Directive   Document of the Federal Reserve providing explicit guidelines for the conduct of monetary policy in the financial markets during the interval between monthly meetings in Washington.

Disintermediation   Net outflow of funds from financial intermediaries, usually savings and loan associations and mutual savings banks, as a result of market interest rates substantially exceeding the rate these institutions can pay their depositors.

Exchange Stabilization Fund   Pool of foreign currencies maintained by the U.S. Treasury for intervention in the exchange markets in support of the dollar.

Federal Funds   Deposits at Federal Reserve Banks which may serve as member bank reserves and form the cornerstone of the nation's short-term money market.

Floating Rate Liabilities   Obligations issued by banks and finance companies with coupon interest rates tied, at a fixed spread, to the yield on a highly liquid short-term instrument, such as a three-month Treasury bill.

International Monetary Fund (IMF)   Autonomous organization established after World War II to maintain an orderly international financial system.

Lagged Reserve Accounting   Method introduced in 1968 wherein Federal Reserve member banks are required in a given statement week to hold reserves against deposit levels prevailing two weeks earlier. Contemporaneous reserve accounting, on the other hand, would require reserves to be held against "this week's" deposits.

Liquidity Preference   Tendency of the public to hold wealth in highly liquid short-term assets, unless rates of return on alternative investments are sufficient to induce diversification.

Matched Book   Transactions engaged in by firms trading U.S. Government securities wherein they sell RPs and lend the funds so acquired by temporarily purchasing securities from another source. As long as they lend at a rate above that at which they borrow, they profit from this operation.

Monetary Base   Member bank reserves plus currency in circulation. It is a key element in the "monetarist" approach to money stock control.

Money Multiplier   The variable relating the monetary base to the money supply. It is dependent upon the public's desire for different types of deposits, the distribution of deposits among banks, and other factors as well, and thus may be difficult to predict in the short run.

Money Supply   Definitions were altered in 1980; herewith are the old and "new" definitions of key aggregates.

> *M*-1 *(old)*   currency plus demand deposits.
>
> *M*-2 *(old)*   M-1 plus time and savings deposits at commercial banks less large CDs plus checkable deposits at thrift institutions.
>
> *M*-3 *(old)*   M-2 plus deposits at thrift institutions.
>
> *M*-4 *(old)*   M-2 plus large negotiable CDs.
>
> *M*-1-A *(new)*   currency plus demand deposits excluding deposits due to foreign banks and official institutions.
>
> *M*-1-B *(new)*   M-1-A plus other checkable deposits at banks and thrift institutions.
>
> *M*-2 *(new)*   M-1-B plus overnight RPs and Eurodollars, money market mutual fund shares, and savings and small time deposits at commercial banks and thrift institutions.
>
> *M*-3 *(new)*   M-2 plus large time deposits and term RPs at commercial banks and thrift institutions.

Open Market Operation   Purchase or sale of U.S. Government securities in the market for such securities by the Federal Reserve.

Operating Factors Factors influencing the quantity of available member bank reserves that are not controlled by the Federal Reserve. The two most important are:

> **Float** Results in double counting of reserve balances because check clearing leads to the crediting of reserves at some banks before the corresponding debiting occurs at others.

> **Treasury Balance** When the Treasury adds to its balances at Federal Reserve banks at the expense of its deposits at commercial banks, a reserve drain occurs. Disbursements by the Treasury from its Federal Reserve balances reverse this and add reserves to the banking system.

Positive Carry The yield premium required by investors to draw them out of very short term investments, say Federal funds, and into longer-dated instruments.

Repurchase Agreement (RP) A short-term transaction wherein the borrower sells the lender a Treasury or Agency security and agrees to buy it back on a specified date at a prearranged price.

Special Drawing Rights International Reserve asset created by the International Monetary Fund for use in settlement of balance of payments gaps or for acquisition of specific foreign currencies.

Swap Network Federal Reserve system of "reciprocal currency arrangements" wherein one country, say the U.S., gains deposits denominated in, say, marks at the Bundesbank in exchange for dollar balances at the New York Federal Reserve. The marks acquired in this fashion can then be used by the Federal Reserve to purchase dollars in the open market or from the Bundesbank, thus helping to support the currency.

Velocity "Income velocity," or the number of times a given money stock must turn over to support a particular level of aggregate spending. For example, if GNP is $2.5 trillion and M-1-B is $400 billion, then the velocity of M-1-B is 6.25.

Yield Curve The relation between yield to maturity and the length of time to maturity of a reasonably homogeneous group of securities.

Index

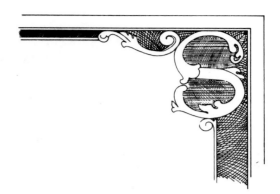